HERE BY
Assignment

The Reverend Archie Ivy Story

A biography by Charles Taylor

Here by Assignment: The Reverend Archie Ivy Story

ISBN: 978-1-09831-871-0

eBook ISBN: 978-1-09831-872-7

DEDICATION

This book is dedicated to folks who have the odds stacked against them, but through grace manage to persevere, lead productive lives and leave the world a better place.

ACKNOWLEDGMENTS

Many people contributed to the completion of this book. First and foremost is Dr. Archie Ivy, who patiently sat through hours and hours of interviews over a five-month period. I would also like to acknowledge the following individuals for their help in making this book possible: Andrea Ivy, Elizabeth Johanna, and Carmen Porco.

I must give a special shout-out to my wife, Camilla who patiently read and helped edit the manuscript, and also to Susanna Daniel, my colleague, who helped draft this book. Susanna is the author of *Stiltsville*, winner of the 2011 PEN/Bingham Award, and *Sea Creatures*, a Target Book Club selection. She is also the cofounder of the Madison Writers' Studio, a high-level private writing workshop in Madison, Wisconsin, and has recently finished her third novel.

CONTENTS

FOREWORD

For many years, the thought of a book about my life has been in the depths of my mind, but taking the time to actually make it happen has been my biggest challenge. When my children were young, I would share with them stories from my life growing up in rural, segregated Shannon, Mississippi, during the forties into the mid-sixties.

We would travel to Shannon yearly when they were youngsters, and I would show them certain sites and landmarks that held a special meaning to me. I would explain to them how I faced the many challenges of being Black and poor in Mississippi and how living this experience helped me to become the person I am today.

Over the years, during Black History Month, I have shared with students in Milwaukee stories from my past to encourage them to have hope in a better future. But I had never, until now, put my life story in writing.

As I have shared my personal journey, three individuals consistently encouraged me to put it into a book. They told me that it would be interesting reading and I hope they're right: Dr. Kirk Byron Jones, a college professor, theologian, teacher, writer, and author of several books; my youngest child, Andrea, who felt that my story should be told; and my good friend Rev. Carmen Porco, who has transformed how low income public housing should be managed in this country.

Carmen and I have been meeting for breakfast monthly over the past five years. As we engaged in conversation, encouraging one another and discussing various subjects and current events, we often discussed our upbringing, life experiences, and family. It was during one of these breakfast meetings that I finally took the idea of having a book written about me seriously.

Carmen introduced me to Dr. Charles Taylor, who has written and produced both documentaries and books. Dr. Taylor was also the author of Carmen's well-received biography. After meeting Dr. Taylor, I agreed to tell my story. We scheduled a series of interviews over many months and I shared my life's journey with him. Charles has great interviewing skills. His probing and challenging questions awoke memories in me that had been buried since childhood.

As I was recalling my life, I didn't realize the emotional roller coaster ride I would experience. Reliving my memories sometimes caused the feelings of anger, sadness, and pain to rise in me. But these conversations with Dr. Taylor also enabled me to better understand, in a positive way, how the difficulties that challenged me in life, in the segregated South and North, helped me to become a man of faith.

I hope my story will demonstrate to folks who have the odds stacked against them, that they, too, can become positive, productive people in life. By sharing some of the things I have experienced and overcome in life, I hope my story will inspire you to strengthen your faith in God.

As a pastor who has devoted his life to Jesus Christ, I believe that God has a plan, a purpose and an assignment for every person born into this world. If you will allow Him, He will work His plan and purpose in your life to carry out the assignment. The Scripture that convinced me of my assignment was 2 Peter 2:10, which says: "Therefore, brethren, be even more diligent to make your call and election sure, for if you do these things you will never stumble."

As the title of this book suggests, I'm *here by assignment*. I hope this book inspires you and touches your spirit. God bless you!

Rev. Dr. Archie L. Ivy

INTRODUCTION

I first met Reverend Archie Ivy while I was working on our mutual friend Reverend Carmen Porco's biography. Carmen showered praise on Archie, calling him a man of God who practiced what he preached: a hard worker with an extraordinary will to succeed. It was obvious there was a great deal of respect between the two of them. As I got to know Reverend Ivy, I found him to be a friendly, humble man, dedicated to his Baptist church ministry.

He sees the church as a place for all people—the embodiment of Christ where church members bring different gifts and abilities. He says "the church must instill hope in people and help them discover a better way of life."

Archie's family, especially his youngest daughter, Andrea, had wanted him to record his memoir for years, and after I agreed to assist, he consented to share his story. I interviewed Archie, his family, and friends over a five-month period. I soon realized that his story would not be about a person who has done extraordinary things, although he has accomplished much, but rather about an ordinary person who has tried to live a godly life and whose example has touched many in profound ways. Archie is not flashy. Indeed, he's just the opposite: quiet, reflective, steady, and a calming presence who knows how to get things done.

In the beginning, it was difficult to get Rev. Ivy to talk about himself. I think he was guarded because he felt people would judge him more harshly as a pastor if he revealed his innermost thoughts. But I reminded him that's why people read biographies—they want to know if you went through the same trials and tribulations that they had to go through; if you faced the same pain and joy in life that they did. As he grew to trust me more, he began to open up, and I began to get a clearer picture of his life's journey.

Archie was born at home, in a shack, on August 17, 1942, in Shannon, Mississippi. He came of age in the Deep South during a time of Klansmen; Colored and White signs in public spaces and with Blacks sitting in the back of the bus. "We knew that at certain places, the front door was for white folks and the back door was for us," says Archie when he recalls his childhood.

He grew up dirt-poor, the oldest of ten children. He moved around a lot as a kid. Archie can remember moving from shack to shack over a dozen times by mule and wagon before he was even a teenager. His father was a sharecropper during those transient years and had to go wherever he could find work. Archie lived in shacks for most of his childhood in the country, a few miles outside of Shannon, without running water and an outhouse in the backyard.

His chores included chopping wood, bringing in the coal, milking cows, feeding the hogs and chickens, and babysitting his younger siblings. As he got older, he worked in the fields planting crops, chopping, and picking cotton. He hauled hay, drove tractors, and worked in a dairy barn. He always did more than his share and learned to be self-reliant at a young age.

While there wasn't much to do in the country, when Archie did have some leisure time, he enjoyed hunting and fishing and playing basketball. He especially enjoyed playing baseball in the cow pastures in the summer. Church life was the culture center for Blacks in Shannon. "Church was all that we had as a people," says Archie. The church was their community, and most of the youth clubs and activities originated from the church. "People in Shannon were segregated by church and race," Archie says. There were different church communities and you were known by the church you attended.

Although the population of Shannon was around 600 when Archie was a kid, Shannon's schools were segregated. He attended the Shannon Colored School which housed all of the town's Blacks in one building—grade K-12.

The wounds from his schooling still haunt him. He was affected deeply by being held back in school, through no fault of his own. The segregated Shannon, Mississippi, schools back then required Black students to pay for the chairs they sat in each year, something white students didn't have to do. When his father refused to do so, the school punished Archie by holding him back a grade. This impacted his life in many ways and partially explains why he is an overachiever, thinking he always has to prove himself to others. He still feels uncomfortable if someone asks him how old he was when he graduated from high school.

Archie says he's always felt different. He didn't follow the crowd and was called "chicken" or "scaredy-cat" by his peers because he avoided getting into trouble in his youth. He accepted Christ and was baptized at the young age of nine years old. He was a good kid, active in his church, and obeyed his parents. His grandma, "Big Mama Ollie," whom Archie says, "loved the Lord," taught him about the Bible, and even as a kid, it was his favorite book to read. His mom made sure he focused on school and taught him math and his ABC's before he started school.

He was the first in his family to attend college, Jackson State University, a historically Black school in Mississippi, about 170 miles from Shannon, where he majored in Industrial Education. This degree would allow him to teach shop classes. He worked his way through college and spent his summers at home in Shannon where he worked as a carpenter with Hosea and George Foster who were brothers in the trade.

He had never been out of Mississippi until he graduated from college. He jumped at the chance to move north to Milwaukee, Wisconsin, to start his teaching career. When Archie arrived in Milwaukee, he soon discovered that Jim Crow had made the journey with him. Milwaukee was then, and remains today, a very segregated city.

His first teaching assignment was at Robert Fulton Middle School, nick-named "Blackboard Jungle" after the film with Sidney Poitier. The school was located in the inner city of Milwaukee and had become a "dumping ground" for troubled Black youth. Archie spent eight years at the school befriending young people and becoming a role model to many of the students there. He served the last four years of his career as the principal at North Division High School where he helped turn things around after gaining the support of parents and teachers. He believes his experience as a teacher helps him as a preacher.

He felt the call to ministry while he was still a teacher but resisted for nearly a decade. He said he wasn't running away from his calling as much as he was trying to make himself acceptable to God. "Once I submitted to God's will, I dedicated my life to Christ," says Archie.

Archie married a woman from Shannon—Jeanette Rogers—who unbeknownst to him had moved to Milwaukee shortly before Archie arrived there. They are blessed with three children and two grandchildren.

Archie's spiritual journey eventually led him to New Hope Missionary Baptist Church in Milwaukee, Wisconsin, where he has been the pastor for nearly 25 years. During his tenure, he has made notable contributions to his church and the larger Milwaukee community. He serves on numerous boards and served a stint as president of MICAH—Milwaukee Inner City Congregation Allied for Hope, an organization that is trying to build a more just society. He has also served as Dean and President of the Wisconsin General Baptist State Congress of Christian Education. He continued his education and now holds both Masters and Doctorate degrees.

Pastor Ivy plans to retire in the next few years, and if he is able to do so, would have achieved a milestone that few modern-day preachers reach.

According to the latest statistics, only 10 per cent of ministers are able to retire from their ministry. A pastor's life is not easy and the burnout rate is extremely high with over 1500 pastors leaving the ministry each month. Yet, Rev. Ivy has persevered and has led his African American church to new heights. He has made New Hope an integral part of Milwaukee's central city. He believes this is the path that God has chosen for him, or as he would say, "I'm here by assignment!"

In writing this book, I discovered that Dr. Ivy is a beloved pastor, a family man, a great teacher, and administrator. His friends and colleagues, such as educators Dr. Howard Fuller and lawyer Cory Nettles, unequivocally profess that he has made a real difference in Milwaukee. Although he came from humble beginnings at a time and place where Blacks were kept from succeeding, he beat the odds.

While he has gone through much of his life feeling out of place, he found refuge in the church. His grandmother played a major role in his young life and gave him the religious grounding that continues to guide his life. Even though he has grievances from his ministry, he is not bitter. He believes that God has a plan and a purpose for each one of us. I'm honored that he allowed me to help tell his story.

Charles Taylor, Author

CHAPTER 1
Mississippi Roots

"I can do all things through Christ which
strengthened me." –Philippians 4:13

There's an old saying: There is the South, and then there is Mississippi. When people think of Mississippi, they think of the murders of Emmett Till, Medgar Evers, the three civil rights workers, Schwerner, Goodman, and Chaney, and thousands of others whose names we will never know. They think of the mob on the Ole' Miss campus in 1962 confronting James Meredith who was simply trying to pursue a higher education.

Like jazz singer Billie Holiday's song, "Strange Fruit," they also think of the 500-plus Blacks who were lynched in that state between 1892 and 1968, the largest number of lynchings in any state. Mississippi was the last state to remove the confederate emblem on its official state flag, having done so in the summer of 2020. Mississippi didn't ratify the Thirteenth Amendment banishing slavery until 2013.

For more than 200 years, the state of Mississippi has used violence and unjust laws to disenfranchise its African American community. Mississippi remains the poorest state in the United States and its Black citizens continue to bear the brunt of that poverty. This was the Mississippi that Archie Lee Ivy was born into.

The civil rights movement had not yet taken hold when Archie was born in rural Shannon, Mississippi. Most rural Blacks were landless sharecroppers or laborers facing inescapable poverty. Archie's family was no different.

Archie was born at home on August 17, 1942, with a white doctor named Dr. Cowden on the scene, along with Archie's grandmother, "Big Mama Ollie," who was known for her skills at midwifery. Blacks were often barred from the white hospitals in Mississippi back then, but white doctors could make house calls if they chose to. The Black infant mortality rate was much higher than whites, so Archie's mom, Ruby, had one more thing to worry about as she labored in pain. Archie is sure she and other family members prayed hard for his safe birth. Fortunately, their prayers were answered and Archie was born a healthy baby.

SHANNON

Shannon is a small town in Lee County in the northeast part of Mississippi about ten miles south of Tupelo, Mississippi. It is surrounded on all sides by lowlands, which made the town feel as if it rose up from the earth like an island from the sea. A cluster of communities that composed Shannon Township are nestled in the lowlands. It is also bordered by the Tombigbee River, which often flooded parts of the town in the spring.

When Archie was born, Shannon had a population of around 600 people. The town is named for Samuel Shannon, who purchased land at that location from the Native American Chickasaw Chief, Itawamba, in the early 1800s. The town grew following the Treaty of Pontotoc, which enabled white settlers to obtain additional Chickasaw land. Shortly afterwards, strawberries were introduced as a cash crop which required a substantial amount of farm laborers.

Shannon became a railroad stop when the railroad company laid tracks through the town in the 1800s. For years, Shannon was widely known as a large strawberry territory, shipping strawberries by railroad cars all over the United States.

Later, landowners built large plantations and introduced cotton, corn, and other crops to the area. All this farm work required cheap workers. There was a settlement of formerly enslaved Black people after the Civil War who came to Shannon to find farm work. Archie's great-great-grandfather and great-great-grandmother, Sam and Martha Trice, put down roots there as freed ex-slaves. Blacks continued to settle in Shannon looking for farm work up to the second migration during WWII.

Until 1956, Shannon's downtown was made up of five general stores, a movie theater, a post office, a furniture factory, a grocery store, a warehouse, a bank, a doctor's office, the city jail, a cotton gin, and the grain elevator. Shannon was mostly rural, and although most of its residents were Black, all the stores were owned by whites.

Shannon like so many railroad towns slowly declined when highways replaced the railroad for personal travel. Its population today is less than 2,000 residents.

SHARECROPPING

Archie's great-great grandparents, just like his parents and grandparents, were sharecroppers. Sharecropping replaced slavery as the main form of work for Blacks in Mississippi after the Civil War. Although Blacks all over the South pleaded for their own land, 40 acres, and a mule from the federal government and for the big plantations to be divided up into small family farms, that request was never granted and sharecropping emerged as the compromise.

It was supposed to be a method for Blacks to work the land and split the earnings from the crops they grew with the landlords. It soon became another way to suppress Blacks when a series of laws and legal interpretations by the courts gave landlords claim to crops over claims by farmers—the crop lien: defined sharecroppers as wage hands rather than tenants; limited share-croppers' ability to contract or move while in debt; and protected creditors' claims for advances to grow the crops.

"We could never get out of debt," said Archie. As a result, they couldn't get out of poverty either.

BLACK CHURCH

There was one institution that Blacks controlled and it was at the center of their lives in Shannon—the Black church. Although Shannon's Black population was less than 300 people while Archie was growing up, there were several Black communities, each with its own church. This included Johnson Chapel Community, where his family lived, the Pine Grove Community, Blackland Community, and the Good Hope Community, into which his future wife was born and raised. The communities were named for the churches that stood there and their social and cultural lives revolved around the church.

"All of our youth clubs, Boy Scouts, baseball, Baptist Young People's Union (BYPU), Baptist Training Union (BTU), and activities for the girls were organized in the church," says Archie. "Church socials, Sunday picnics, Bible study, and praise meetings all were church sponsored and created a social cohesion, a tight-knit community that nurtured hope in the face of discrimination and violence."

Archie's family was a loyal member of the church and it was there that Archie obtained his spiritual grounding. "We always walked to and from church," Archie says. "It was about a mile or so each way. The congregation was made up of families, not even 100 people-maybe 75, or around there. Now it's much larger and people come from all over."

The church was one of the few places where he felt he fit in. "This was my safe haven. I knew I could always depend on God. It didn't matter how my day went or the hardships we had to go through because I could always count on the Lord."

WWII

Nine months before Archie's birth, the Japanese had bombed Pearl Harbor, drawing the U.S. into WWII. Mississippi responded with unbridled patriotism and thousands of Mississippians, including Blacks, joined the armed services. Many of Archie's cousins and uncles fought in the war, although his father, Mose, did not. Many Mississippi plantation owners feared the Federal War Manpower Commission (WMC) would create a labor shortage of low-wage workers if they allowed too many Blacks to join the army, since most farmworkers were Black.

Southern plantation owners were successful in getting a law passed that moved control of farm labor from the WMC to the US Department of Agriculture, a government agency that they controlled at the state level. No longer would there be an agency to help Black farmworkers find jobs off the plantation. Landowners controlled the local draft boards as well so they weren't about to let Blacks like Mose, Archie's father, be drafted when they intended to exploit him and other Blacks to work their lands.

When the US government rationed goods, Shannon's Blacks who were barely scraping by suffered even more. Although Shannon was not a military base during the war, many places in Mississippi were. Black soldiers from the north came down for training and racial tension increased in every city they were stationed in. Many protested the local conditions and their resistance, no doubt, affected local Blacks.

When Black soldiers returned from the war, many were upset with the racist status quo and started petitioning for civil rights for Black people. Although Mississippi was still in last place among the states in terms of per capita income, ironically, the war effort raised the standard of living for whites. It also ushered in an era of mechanization for the agricultural industry which put many Black sharecroppers out of work.

Shannon was less affected than other towns because it had little ties to the war front. As a result, Mose was still able to find jobs on the farm but it meant he had to be willing to move from farm to farm based on local needs. This took a heavy toll on his family and other Black sharecroppers.

There has never been a time in America when Black children were born with a cleared path toward success the way many white children are, with generational wealth passed onto them and without the oppressive force of institutional racism limiting their opportunities and crushing their spirit. Archie was born during a particularly shameful time in this country's history, when Jim Crow was still alive and well, when even survival was a long shot for many Black families.

But there were bright spots and life lessons available to Archie throughout his childhood. The way his family moved from shack to shack, with all the mouths to feed and children to watch over, instilled in Archie a deep sense of responsibility that maybe he would not have learned in a household with fewer challenges. It taught him to value the homestead, the people in it, and the work it takes to keep it going. It also showed him through real life experience what he wanted for his future and the future of any family he might have. He wanted his children to take for granted the kind of stability that he had never experienced as a child, and he wanted them to access the level of education and self-determination that had been so difficult for him to find for himself.

Shannon, including the sharecropping life that kept his family from growing roots in any given home, and the constant presence of so many siblings, cousins, aunts and uncles, grandparents, and others–this was the world where Archie not only developed his sense of dependability and hard work, it was also the context in which he was initiated into his lifelong relationship with God.

Archie's parents had lived hard lives. He knew this even as a young child, and he knew they worked and sacrificed everything they could to make sure their children had what they needed, that they had food and clean clothes and a roof over their heads.

Far too many Blacks in Mississippi during this time worked themselves into the grave in fields, hoeing and weeding and harvesting, doing their best but falling short. So many Blacks worked in homes, cleaning and cooking and caring for white children, praying that their own children would not grow up to find themselves doing the same back-breaking labor, hoping that through education, their children might have opportunities that had been denied to Blacks since the founding of this country.

Archie was born into and grew up in a world filled with racial tensions and violence, widespread white supremacy, rabble-rousing racist politicians, and laws that made sure Blacks couldn't make any gains for themselves.

He also grew up in a church community that was filled with acts of love, kinship, grace, and dignity that never turned its back on their relationship with the Lord.

It's possible that another person raised in Archie's circumstances, with its limited opportunities and unfair burdens, might have become bitter. In the 2014 documentary, *Freedom Summer,* there's an apt line spoken by a young activist: "A Black man in Mississippi who ain't angry ain't been pay'n attention!"

Surely, many of Archie's family members and neighbors were angry, as they had every right to be, and although Archie says he was not bitter, he was most definitely paying attention, then and now. He is acutely aware of how the hardships of his upbringing impacted his life. And it wouldn't be honest to say he has no anger—at Jim Crow, at wage and housing disparities, and at a current President who knowingly stokes racism at a time when we need to come together as a nation.

But anger is not the force that has led Archie to become a "man of God." What has made him successful are the forces that helped him control and make use of his anger, like his thoughtfulness, his refusal to argue disagreeably, his extensive reading and study that formed his sophisticated intellect, and his pride in who he is, flaws and all.

Archie was paying attention and he understands how his past has helped shape his present. Mississippi was his roots but his grandmother Ollie taught him that heaven was his destination.

CHAPTER 2

Childhood

"But seek ye first the kingdom of God, and his righteousness; and all these things shall be added unto you." –Matthew 6:33

Archie came from a big family, which was not unusual in the South during the 40s and 50s. He was the oldest of ten children born to Mose and Ruby Ivy, both of whom came from large families themselves. Mose, who grew up in Prairie Point, Mississippi, in Picking County, was one of seven children. Mose dropped out of school in third grade and left home at around age thirteen to work for a white Shannon businessman named Gus Johnson. Gus lived in the Johnson Chapel community and operated a country store, but his side business was where he made his real money: selling *moonshine*, which was a kind of corn whiskey. Since Gus offered him a job, Mose decided that he would put down stakes in Shannon.

It was common in those days for a white person to have a Black person work for them around the house or on the farm, doing odd jobs, like a butler or house boy. Mose wasn't forced, but he wasn't paid well, either. Gus Johnson called him "Af," which was short for African. Archie recalls his father selling moonshine right out of the house sometimes.

"My father was good at making moonshine," said Archie, "and along with Gus Johnson, they made a *lot* of it."

Mose met Ruby Ella Edmond in Shannon around 1940. Ruby was the youngest of five, and her parents were Ollie and Arch Edmond. Throughout Archie's childhood, Ollie, who everyone called Mama Ollie, was the grandparent who affected the deepest part of Archie's character for many reasons, not the least of which was that she introduced him to the book that would profoundly change his future: The Holy Bible.

Ruby was 14 years old when she and Mose started courting, and on May 7, 1941, when she was 16, they married. Mose was 23. Back then, it was common place for men to marry younger women, especially in poor communities in the South. By the time they married, Mose had branched out from moonshine and was also working as a sharecropper. This enabled the couple to settle right outside of Shannon proper, in the country. Within a year, Ruby was pregnant with Archie, her firstborn. Mose's father was named Archie Ivy and Ruby's father was named Arch Edmond, so Archie's name came from both of his grandfathers.

Archie's sister, Ollie, was born twenty-two months later, on June 27, 1944. Between Ollie and the next boy, Joe, who was born October 7, 1946, there was a baby boy named Fred, who died of Sudden Infant Death Syndrome when he was just ten months old. Archie was too young to remember him.

"Every time I looked up, my mom was pregnant again," Archie said about this time of his life.

When Archie and Ollie were small, the family lived in a two-bedroom shack on property that belonged to their uncle, Spencer Jackson, who was Mama Ollie's brother-in-law. This was where Archie spent the most carefree years of his childhood, where at age three and four, he ran, laughed, and played in the yard in short pants with his sister and playmate, tumbling and breathing in the smells of the season.

One of Archie's earliest memories happened on the walk home from church one night. On this particular walk, maybe because the kids were extremely tired, his father was carrying him and his mother was carrying Ollie.

"That's the only time I can remember my father holding or hugging me," said Archie. "He never told me he loved me, either. I never disrespected him; I always obeyed him, never talked back. My father wasn't the type of man who expressed his feelings much."

It would be years before Archie would become aware of any tension between his parents. Theirs was not a violent home by any means, and there was only one time that Archie ever showed his father any anger. It happened a decade later. One Saturday after a baseball game, Mose was drinking heavily and he and Ruby started to push and hit each other. Archie felt an intense anger and jumped between the two of them.

"I shouted never to raise a fist to my mother again, and as far as I know, he never did," said Archie.

About the time his brother, Joe, was born, the family moved into a three-room house owned by Joe Clarke, a white banker who hired Mose as a sharecropper. Then Archie's sister Mamie was born on April 18, 1949, when Archie was about to turn six. When Mamie was a baby, she was bitten on the lip by a rat while she was sleeping, which gave the family a terrible scare. The doctor came and prescribed medicine to help her recover, but Archie says if you look closely today, you can still see a small scar. "The houses we lived in were really shacks with tin roofs and rats in the walls," Archie quietly reveals.

When Archie's parents worked in the fields, Archie and his siblings played on a pallet in the shade with their dog, Dumpy, a German Shepherd-Collie mix who let the kids roll around on him yet growled at any strangers who came too close. Archie has many good memories of time spent on that pallet feeling carefree and happy. This was well before he was old enough to take part in the responsibilities of running the home and babysitting his younger siblings.

After Mamie was born, the family had two girls and two boys.

"I thought mom and dad were done having babies then," said Archie, chuckling.

He was wrong, of course. Mary was born on March 21, 1951. Archie was nine years old at this time, mature enough to learn how to change diapers and babysit. His help became essential right away, because when Mary was still a toddler, Mose and some of his friends temporarily left Shannon to find work on the railroads up north in Gary, Indiana. Without the sharecropping to tether them to a house, Ruby moved Archie and his four siblings into one room in the home of her parents, Mama Ollie and Papa Arch. "We had the room back behind the kitchen," Archie recalls.

Archie remembers living with his grandparents vividly, because this was the time when he first felt the call to serve God. It was also a time of bonding with his Papa Arch, who gave Archie small tasks to do around the house and in his Blacksmith shop. Archie was growing up, learning more about what it meant to take care of a house and family, and even learning new skills. He also loved being outside with his many cousins playing baseball. His love of baseball would turn out to last a lifetime, and it had its origins in scrub lots around Shannon, where he and his friends put together teams and spent hours playing in the hot sun.

There was never enough time for baseball, though. Never enough time for friends or being idle or exploring. Since Archie was the oldest, most of the household responsibilities fell on his shoulders. Archie had to babysit several hours a day, as well as take care of other chores. There was no shortage of work to be done around the house. Before they had a gas stove, they used wood to cook and heat the house. Many years just before winter hit, Archie would go with Mose to cut down trees for firewood and haul it back to the house. He was in charge of keeping the fire going inside, and when they owned animals, he milked the cows and made sure the hogs were fed.

"I also used to stand on a stool in the kitchen and help Mother cook. Of course, after we ate, I'd wash the dishes. My inside chores included mopping the floors, getting water from the well behind the house, and heating up the baths and laundry. I wasn't working in the fields yet—that would come a few years later—but the work of the family home was a powerful lesson in growing up fast."

The twins, Jesse and Jack, were born April 24, 1954. Ruby and Mose named them for the white doctor who came to the house to deliver them, Dr. Rommie Grafton Dabbs, and the doctor's wife, Jesse. This was Dr. Dabbs' first delivery of twins, so he suggested naming them after himself and his wife. My brother Jessie was given Dabbs' wife's first name and my brother, Jack, received Dr. Dabbs' middle name.

A year later, on July 15, 1955, Mose O'Neal Ivy was born. Mose Sr. had left his railroad work for good by this time, and now the family was living in a shack on the same property as Arch and Ollie, sharecropping for a man named Keith Bonnett.

Ruby retired from having children after Mose Jr. was born—but only for nine years. On December 7, 1964, when Archie was 22 years old, along came the last child, Darlene.

In the eighteen years of Archie's childhood, the family lived in more than a dozen different shanties. But every one of them was located within the confines of the town of Shannon, and all ten kids were born and raised there. Although the family did not have the kind of stability where they were all born and raised to adulthood in the same house, they did have a different kind of stability: a community where they always knew everyone

13

and everyone knew them; a church they attended year after year; friends and family they could depend on and who depended on them.

Archie and his siblings rode a country bus to Shannon's colored school, which took a route that passed by the white school. The white school's facilities were much newer and well-kept, and the colored school received the white school's hand-me-downs.

"At our school, we only had two sports, and that was basketball and softball," said Archie. "There was no gymnasium when I was in grade school, and the building didn't get one until 1960. The kids played outside instead. The white school, on the other hand, had football, basketball, baseball, track and field, and their own well-equipped gym."

When Archie attended school, there was only one building for Black students and it housed all grades, plus a separate agricultural and home economics classroom. He and his classmates started out on one side of the building, then moved up the same side of the building until they reached seventh grade, at which point they went to the other side of the building. In the early 60s, a new building was erected, and that was the high school. The original building became the elementary school, named for Rev. E.L. Siggers, a Methodist pastor and the principal, a graduate of Morehouse College in Atlanta, GA.

Archie's childhood was richly populated by his siblings and their likes and dislikes, and habits and complaints. Ollie, for example, was the tomboy of the family. She revered Archie but usually got his attention the wrong way: by telling on him and trying to get him into trouble at home. At school, she roped him into defending her in fights with other kids. Joe also tended to be a troublemaker, adventurous, and mischievous. Once, Archie received a BB gun for Christmas, which he treasured. Joe accidently destroyed the gun by putting matchsticks inside it. This was the kind of sibling prank not easily forgotten.

Mamie was the smart one, Archie recalls. Like him, Mamie, Joe, and Mary would all end up graduating from high school, though Archie would be the only one to graduate from college. Archie always figured Mamie was a shoe-in for college, but instead, she married young and took a job working in textiles.

The twins, Jesse and Jack, were not identical, but together with their youngest brother, Mose, formed a threesome throughout their childhood. "They were so close in age and in spirit that people often mistook them for triplets."

No matter how many children lived at home at any given time, no matter which shack they happened to be living in, there were never more than two bedrooms. The close quarters meant that everyone had to keep their tempers and try to get along. They made do in the small space by sleeping at least four kids to one bed.

"I slept at the head of the bed sometimes, and the girls slept at the foot. Usually, Joe and I crammed together," said Archie. When the twins came along, the family converted a front porch into an extra room.

The year that Archie received a BB gun for Christmas, his sister Ollie received a doll that made a noise when you squeezed it. Archie was five years old that year, and he was fascinated by how things worked. In an effort to figure it out, he performed surgery on the doll using kitchen tools. He hadn't really considered that what he was doing was wrong, but he soon learned it was.

"I got a whipping and my sister had a fit."

"It was Christmas, 1948," Archie recalls. He received a BB gun and was outside shooting it off with one of his uncles, Tom Henry, whom everyone called Brit. For reasons young Archie didn't understand, his uncle Brit told him to leave the lever down after cocking the gun, then pull the trigger. This wasn't how the gun was supposed to work, Archie knew, but he trusted his uncle Brit. He shouldn't have. The lever closed on his hand when he pulled the trigger, breaking the skin. That day, he learned not only how not to use a BB gun but to be careful whom you trust.

That same Christmas, Archie was given a red wagon. He assumed when he received it that it would be for playing, but quickly learned it was meant to help him do his chores. It was useful for hauling wood and the five-gallon water jug from the well, for the washing, bathing, and cooking. At one time, they lived in a place where three families shared the same well. Throughout his entire upbringing in Shannon, the family never had indoor plumbing, only outhouses out back. In the sweltering heat of the summers, they used sticks to prop open the windows in the hopes of catching a passing breeze preferably not in the direction of the outhouse.

"I learned to iron and wash clothes as a kid. I heated the water to bathe and used a washboard. We boiled the clothes and hung them on a line and if they didn't fit on the clothesline, we'd hang the rest on the fence," said Archie about his chore-filled childhood.

Christmas became a special event by the time Archie reached the age of twelve. He was given the responsibility to help place special toys under the tree for his younger siblings.

Trains passed through the parts of Shannon where the family once lived, and Archie played a game with himself of counting the boxcars. He wondered where the trains came from and where they went, and he yearned to get on one and discover the answers for himself. One day, when he was about six or seven years old, he got his wish. His parents made plans for him and his sister Ollie to take the train to visit Mose's mother, Big Momma Mamie, in Prairie Point, Mississippi, which was about seventy miles away. This was a world away in Archie's eyes, since at the time he'd never been farther than Tupelo.

They packed their bags and got dressed in their Sunday clothes. Viola, Mose's youngest sister, was going to travel with them. Archie was so excited he could hardly keep still. They waited with the other passengers for the train to pull into the station and the doors to open. They couldn't wait to find their seats and feel the pull of the train as it rolled out of the station and left Shannon behind.

But they had to wait. And wait some more. They were forced to board last, and then they were made to sit in the colored section of the train.

Like most people, Archie's childhood was full of new experiences and excitement, but it was also shaded by the constant reminder that Blacks were secondary citizens, especially when traveling in Mississippi. He hadn't known what this really meant before, and now he did. Every new experience held a lesson in humiliation and oppression.

In Prairie Point, Archie and his sister played with their cousins at Big Mama Mamie's house, and life felt right to Archie. But then they returned home on the train, last to board and assigned to the colored section, and traveling never quite seemed so enticing again.

Once Archie and his siblings were older, Mose left moonshine behind and shifted his focus to sharecropping and then to working at the grain elevator in town. This was hard and hazardous work. Workers in grain elevators were known to suffer accidents or even fatalities due to fires, suffocation in storage bins, falls from great heights, and crushing by equipment. And Mose was a serious drinker in those days, which only made him less safe at work and at home. In fact, when Archie was about seven years old, a doctor told Mose that if he didn't quit drinking altogether, it would kill him sooner rather than later.

Mose didn't quit, but Archie doesn't judge him for it. He was a man who carried a heavy burden, but he had dignity and a keen sense of responsibility, says Archie.

"He did the best he could, given the hand God had dealt him. He always looked out for his family, always provided for us. We always had food on the table and never went to bed hungry. Though he never hugged me or told me he loved me, he would surprise me by often repeating that I could do anything I applied my mind to," said Archie.

When Archie thinks back on his childhood, he recalls the resourcefulness of his people. On the same trip when he took the train to Prairie Point to visit his kinfolk, he was playing cutting wood with an axe, and the axe slipped. It cut a gash in his forearm that's visible to this day. Instead of taking him to the doctor, which the family could not afford, Big Momma Mamie gathered soot from the stove pipe, mixed it with turpentine, and applied it to the wound, then bandaged it up.

"My family was pretty self-sufficient. Growing up, they'd make tea from cow chips and we'd drink it to kill a cold or a fever. We used a lot of home remedies, like sassafras tea, castor oil, and rock candy. We'd put goose grease and a warm compress on our chest when we had a cold."

These are examples of how so many Black families used their own resources and knowledge to survive, because medical treatment for Blacks, even when lives were at stake, was never a certainty. Medical treatment that couldn't be taken care of at home existed at the mercy of a particular doctor, and whether that doctor was willing to make house calls and was inclined to do it.

One exception was when white nurses would come to the community to immunize kids under an oak tree at the side of the road. The white nurses were sent there by the county. This was the time of polio, as well as tetanus and other standard vaccines, and the kids would line up and wait for their turns.

"I hated getting shots, says Archie. "Afterwards, we still had to go to the field and hoe, sore arm and all. There was a nurse called Mrs. Wilson, and when it was my turn to get my shot, I ran. This made her mad, and she ran after me and brought me back and gave me my shot. This lady remembered me until she died. Years later when she worked at the clinic, she'd asked my mom about me."

Around age fourteen, Archie added fieldwork to his long list of responsibilities. He helped with the planting in the spring and picking cotton, corn, and other produce. He also hired himself out to chop and pick cotton when white landowners needed extra help during harvest time.

By the time he was sixteen, his father had given up sharecropping entirely and was working steady hours at the grain elevator. All of the older siblings, Ollie, Joe, Mamie, and Mary, were engaged in farm work after school and in the summers. Ruby would take time away from doing domestic work to help gather the crops in the fall. She'd leave the little kids on a pallet in the shade nearby while they worked, just like she'd done when Archie was a little boy.

"The little ones never ended up doing any farming," Archie recalls. "They didn't experience what the rest of us did growing up. I was the head of the family during their childhoods, because my father was off working and the farming was left to us."

When his father left for work in the north, Archie really gained an understanding of what sharecropping was about. He discovered that there were two types of sharecroppers in Shannon: The first type was a person who rented the land from the landowner. This sharecropper had to buy their own seed and fertilizer and plant the crops. At harvest time, the sharecropper would pay one-fourth of the harvest to the landowner.

The second type of sharecropper was a person who lived in a house on the property of the landowner. The landowner would open an account at a local general store in the name of the sharecropper. The landowner provided the funds for all the necessary supplies needed to plant the crop. It was the sharecropper's responsibility to prepare the soil, plant the seed, tend the crop (cultivating, hoeing), and at harvest time, gather the crop, at which time the landowner produced the receipts of all expenses. After deducting the expenses, any remaining profit was divided in half. Which in most instances, left the sharecropper in debt to the owner and forced him to work another year as a sharecropper.

"Maybe that's why we moved around so much," speculates Archie. "My father kept an account of all expenses, and if his numbers and the owners didn't agree, he would make a deal with another landowner and move on.

Archie's memories of his childhood, even though he was dirt poor and Blacks faced racial animosity on a daily basis, are mostly fond. This was, in part, due to the fact that he had a large extended family who served as a support group for each other.

During summers, his siblings and cousins would play together outside, usually at Mama Ollie's and Papa Arch's house. They made their own toys and games, and at times, they made balls from old socks and played baseball in the pasture. Some days, there might have been as many as twenty grandchildren out there spending time together.

"We were barefoot all summer long, saving our Sunday shoes," Archie laughs, remembering some of the best times of his childhood.

Archie was in the Boy Scouts from age twelve through his late teens, and it was with his troop that he learned to camp outdoors, make a fire and pitch a tent, though he'd inherited his love for the outdoors from his father. His father was quite the outdoorsman and loved fishing, hunting, farming, and just being outside.

There were about twelve or fifteen boys in his troop, all Black, and the Boy Scout leader was Archie's cousin by marriage, Hosea Foster. It was in the Scouts that Archie first learned how to play baseball officially, rules and all. It was also one of Archie's early experiences with fellowship and leadership, both of which would become mainstays of his life in many forms.

"I loved camping and being with not only the boys in our community but from other communities, too," Archie said.

He also loved to go fishing. He and his siblings would pile into the back of his Papa Arch's truck and go down to the various creeks and small lakes. They caught bluegill, croppy, bass, and catfish—lots of catfish—and Archie's father Mose, made nets for the neighbors and taught Archie how to gut and clean a fish. Sometimes all the cousins would get together and they would have one heck of a fish fry. The kids would play games while the adults would cook and socialize.

Disappointments during Archie's childhood were few, but they stung and left their mark: memories of the train ride sitting in the back, seeing "white only" signs as they passed businesses along the way, and being held back in school. Mostly, the times when Archie was unhappy or frustrated revolved around being tied to the housework and fieldwork, and not having a bike of his own to ride to places with friends.

"We were poor, but mostly we were happy. We never went hungry and my clothes were always clean. I had two pairs of pants and three shirts, so I always knew what I was going to wear. On Sunday, I wore my Sunday pants and my white shirt. But man, it would have been nice to have a bike when I was a kid and a car when I was a teenager," Archie adds.

Rarely did it snow during the 1940s and '50s in Mississippi. If it did, everything closed, though there was freezing rain, sleet, and hail causing ice to form on the trees and power lines. Many years, there were spring floods that overwhelmed the banks of the Tombigbee River and stranded many families in their homes. When it flooded, some teachers and students couldn't make it to the school buildings, and everything stopped for a few days until the water receded.

"When the river rose up high, we couldn't go to school because we couldn't cross the area that the creeks flowed through. Most springs we'd have floods and be out of school for days," he recalled.

When he considers his childhood in Shannon, the poverty and the heavy workload and the many siblings and relatives who populate his memories, Archie spares himself no pity. Without a childhood like the one that formed him, would he have learned survival skills and developed a work ethic like the one that's made him who he is? Would he have learned to hold his head high and be proud of who he is?

"I have always known that I am somebody because I am a child of God!" replies Archie.

CHAPTER 3

School Years

"For we walk by faith, not by sight." –2 Corinthians 5:7

O ne of the most significant events of Archie's young life happened before he started first grade. He was held back two grades in school, between pre-kindergarten and kindergarten. In those days when you started school, you would begin in the pre-primer, then the primer, and then move on to first grade. At least that's what happened for most people.

"I think the first time I was held back, it was because of attendance. We had to walk to school because the school bus did not come back into the area where we lived. It was about a mile or so away, which was a lot for a small kid," said Archie by way of explanation.

The second time, though, was about money.

"We had to buy our own chairs to sit in at school, and there were club dues as well. One day, my father was talking about the fees with Joe Clarke, the town banker. We were living on his place at that time. Mr. Clarke told my dad that there were no fees to be paid at the white school. This really stuck in my father's craw. If whites didn't have to pay, then neither would he. So, he refused to pay, and the school called his bluff, and I was held back a grade."

His mother, Ruby, had taught Archie to read at home, and by this time, he knew the Dick and Jane books by heart, as well as portions of the Bible, which had been pressed into his hand by Big Mama more times than he can recall.

"My mother put up a piece of cardboard with shoe polish alphabet letters, and that was my chart. She taught me how to read and count to 100 before I started school. You had to know math and how to read as a sharecropper, so you didn't get cheated."

There was something else Archie noticed around this time of his life. People were treated differently depending on what their parents did for a living. There were kids whose families were better off financially who were allowed to advance, or even skip grades, and it had nothing to do with brains or studying.

For example, Archie's first cousin, whose family owned their land, never seemed to have the same obstacles placed in her path that he and other poor Black kids did.

"She was two years older than I was but four years ahead in school. Yet, I could read her books and do some of her assignments. If your parents had standing, you were special." Now Archie was exposed to both racism and classism, and the visible signs of both were deeply disturbing to him.

Being held back hurt Archie's pride and his confidence. It also dampened his spirit around age twelve as he was far outpacing his classmates in his growth spurt.

"It was embarrassing, because I was in a class in which most of the kids were two years younger than I was, and I felt like I didn't fit. I knew I was intelligent but people looked at me differently, like I was dumb. I never felt ashamed, exactly, but I felt uncomfortable. People I started school with graduated two years before I did. When I finally graduated from high school, I was twenty years old."

Where would he be now if he hadn't been held back? It's a question Archie still asks himself today at seventy-seven years old.

"I would say that maybe I'm exactly where God designed me to be, even with the disappointments. But it left a bitter taste in my mouth, and I've never gotten over it. Mostly, I blame the system, growing up in a segregated society. 'Separate but equal' they said, but there was no equal. Even today, things are not equal."

By age fourteen, Archie was hiring himself out chopping cotton for $2-$3 per day in the spring, and $3 per hundred pounds for picking cotton in the fall. At the age of sixteen, he began to hire himself out hauling hay for $5 per day and driving tractors. He was making money, but not as much as the white guys who worked alongside him doing the same work.

"I was never that good at picking cotton, but I did it anyway," says Archie about farming. All the money he made went toward clothes and supplies for school. After a year or so, he also started working at the dairy barn, making $7 per week. He never saw any of the money he made because it went straight to his household.

"I was afraid of disappointing my parents, but I made up my mind early that I wasn't going to pick cotton for the rest of my life," Archie recalls.

Once, he and his cousins were picking cotton, helping their grandfather, Papa Arch. "I stood up to rest my back and was looking up into the sky and Papa saw me and asked what I was doing. I told him I was resting my back. He said, "You don't have one yet."

"I didn't understand until much later what he meant," said Archie when he looked back on this memory. "Here I was complaining about picking some cotton and he and his peers had toiled in the fields for years underpaid, overworked without anyone to complain to but God."

In high school, Archie excelled in his history and math classes. He had several teachers who guided and influenced him, including Mrs. Iola Henderson, who took a special interest in him early and never let him get away with anything. "There was the day that I had my first fight at school during lunch period. When we returned to class, Mrs. Henderson, as if she was my mother, made me sit in a chair and gave me a whipping. By the way, the other boy did not receive any punishment." It was Mrs. Henderson who first told Archie that she believed he was headed for college. "She always referred to me as her boy," Archie recalled.

"She and her husband were killed in a car accident my second year of college," he recounted sadly. "She was my favorite teacher. I will never forget the influence she had on my life. Sometimes, all it takes is to have one person who believes in you to keep you going forward."

There was also Mr. Holloway, an agriculture teacher. He, too, told Archie he was going places. And A.J. Fielder, a basketball coach who carried himself in a way that Archie wanted to emulate. "He was a sharp dresser and he flew in the 82nd Airborne Division during WWII. I thought for a while that if I couldn't go to college, I would go into the Air Force."

Then there was Paul Shack, the person who replaced Mr. Fielder as teacher and basketball coach, who told Archie to "aim for the stars." Archie carries these words with him to this day.

Archie also looked up to Rev. E.L. Siggers, his high school principal, as a role model. Rev. Siggers assumed multiple roles, including being Shannon's Methodist pastor and a Morehouse graduate.

"Anyone older than I was, I showed respect. But I could always tell that there were people who were hypocritical, people who said one thing and did another."

One man who always earned Archie's love and respect was his mother's first cousin's husband, Hosea Foster, who was also his Boy Scout troop leader. Hosea was a carpenter and contractor and had served in the military. Archie worked with Hosea and his brothers, George and Phillip, whenever he had the opportunity, including two of his three summers home from college. Hosea would give Archie challenging jobs and assignments while teaching him life lessons.

The Foster boys demanded your best work. Once he was working with George and built a frame for some kitchen cabinets. George inspected the frame, then took a hammer and tore it down while growling, "Do it over."

"He taught me that if I wanted to do a job, I needed to focus, have a plan and do it right," Archie said. "The Foster brothers taught me so many great skills and even today, when I'm working on a project, I think to myself, will it meet their approval?"

And the person who perhaps had the most lasting influence beyond his teenage years was Big Mama Ollie, who not only taught him about God and the Bible but also about Black history and the inventions and talents of African Americans, lessons Rev. Siggers would repeat to him during his school years.

"Despite all of the messages from white people about us, I still became proud of who I was and proud of my people."

As a child Archie wanted a bike more than anything. His parents simply couldn't afford one for him, so he holds no grudges, even though he speaks of the time with pain in his voice. "I never begged anyone to ride their bike," he said "but if they let me ride it, I would be off."

He learned to ride on his cousin's bike, which had no brakes.

"One day I climbed on and coasted straight into a barbed wire fence. I got tangled up and have a scar on my shoulder to this day," he recalled. His cousins sometimes flaunted their bikes to remind him of what he was missing, but Archie's response was to ignore them. All the boys in his neighborhood, it seemed to Archie at the time, had bikes—so they would ride, and he would walk. It was another way of not fitting in. Sometimes, he'd wait to be picked up and his ride would never come, and the next day, his friends would be talking about what they did the night before.

He may not have had a bike, but he did have access to a mule he used in the field. He talks with a great deal of pride in his voice when he describes the day he switched from using a mule in the field to driving a tractor. Driving anything was a big deal for teenagers, and at thirteen, he was able to drive the tractor to take the cotton and the corn to the grain elevator. He felt on top of the world.

"Maybe it doesn't seem like a big thing," Archie said, "but for me, it was a huge step."

Archie didn't date much as a teenager, but he was popular with the girls and their parents. He said his lack of transportation prohibited him from taking girls out. Archie's dates with Minnie, a girl he courted, had to involve a friend who would pick him up and drop him off. Many times, he would have to walk home or he'd have to hitch a ride home from his cousin's café.

Archie said his sister was allowed to date at fourteen. However, the only way she was allowed to go out on a date was that he went along. Her boyfriend, Andrae, was older than she was and had a car, so that was a mode of transportation for movies and such. Archie's cousin, Carl Trice, who was a couple of years younger than Archie, had a car, and Johnny Foster had a car, and sometimes during the week, they would all drive to ball games or dances. Archie could only go if someone picked him up. Eventually, he'd been so disappointed by friends who forgot or neglected to pick him up that he just stayed home reading.

Archie was in high school when the family bought their first car, a Nash. To get his license, Archie practiced driving his parent's car on country roads to and from church or up to the store, never on the highway. All the cars were standard stick shifts and he trained on his Papa Arch's truck until he could avoid grinding the clutch. His father didn't even drive before that time, and when the family got their first car, it was Archie's mother who learned to drive and got her license.

Archie took his driver's test on his parent's second car, a blue and white 1955 Ford, and passed the first time.

"The guy told me he shouldn't have passed me because my hygiene wasn't what it should have been, but of course that had nothing to do with driving," said Archie. "Besides, I had worked in the fields all morning," Archie says laughing.

For the most part, Archie said he was a straight-and-narrow teenager, the kind of kid parents wanted their daughters to date, never disrespectful to his elders or women. Once or twice, he rebelled against his holier instincts and drank too much, but then he was sick and never did it again.

On another occasion, he and some friends went to a dance in Tupelo about ten miles from Shannon, and Archie drove home because he was the only one who was sober. On the way out of town, he was pulled over by the police for taking off too fast from a stop light. He was driving his mother's 1959 Pontiac at the time. He stopped and got out, and the police had him sit on the trunk of the car and answer questions, then eventually told him to go home.

That was one night that he was truly glad that he hadn't drank too much. Archie believes it was divine intervention because rarely did white police officers let a Black person go without a citation. Being Black and driving intoxicated in Mississippi in the late '50s is something you wanted to avoid at all costs.

Of all the sports that Archie played as a teenager, baseball continued to be his favorite. "In the Boy Scouts and in the community, we had a pretty good baseball team. We used to play adult men, and beat them in a sixteen-inning game. I could field, I could hit, and I was pretty fast," Archie boasted. "After church, I'd hide my gear in the bushes and sneak off to get picked up so I could play down in Tupelo."

Shannon didn't have an official baseball field, so Archie and his friends put down bases and made a field in the cow pastures.

"I usually led off the batting order or hit second behind John Hersey, but just before I left for college, I started batting cleanup. If I was in the outfield, nothing hit the ground," claims Archie.

Because baseball was one sport he excelled at and was allowed to play, it had a deep impact on Archie's young life. Although Black athletes had been playing in what was called the Negro Leagues since the 1880s, it wasn't until 1947 when Archie was just five years old that the Major League acquired its first Black player. That was the year that Jackie Robinson started playing first base for the Brooklyn Dodgers.

"That's why baseball was our favorite past time, because Jackie Robinson had made it to the big times," said Archie.

While the Brooklyn Dodgers was the local favorite team in the Black community, his father's favorite team was the Yankees, a team that didn't acquire a Black player until Elston Howard in 1955, after Willie Mays had joined the Giants and Hank Aaron had been drafted by the Milwaukee Braves. Archie knew growing up that although there were a lot of great baseball players around, even in Shannon, it took a special person to endure what Jackie Robinson went through.

"Other Black players might not have made it, but Jackie's attitude was different," said Archie. "It took a certain kind of person to persevere while being spat on, while being separated from his team at hotels, and remaining defiant against racial inequality as he stood on the playing field. Jackie went through so much just to be the first. He prepared a place at the table for others who came after him. I've always admired him for that." Jackie Robinson once said, "A life is not important except in the impact it has on other lives." There's no question that Robinson's life had wide-ranging impact, including on Archie's life.

Around the same time that Jackie Robinson broke the baseball color barrier, boxer Joe Louis was making history as the world heavyweight champion. The Ivy family didn't own a television until around 1960, so they used to gather around the radio and listen to the gospel and baseball games and, memorably, the fights with Joe Louis.

"The announcer would call the fight blow-by-blow, and we all cheered and celebrated. To my father and my grandfather, Louis was an icon because he was a winner and he represented us in the boxing ring. Anyone who could represent our race and dominate was a hero to us. If Joe Louis could do it, then someone else could do it, too. Among Black folk in those years, Joe Louis and Jackie Robinson were heroes. They let us know we were making progress as Black people."

Baseball was the main past time during the summers of Archie's childhood, but he and his friends would also go to the movies and hang out at each other's houses.

"We had a theater in Shannon for a while. It showed one movie at a time and it was segregated. Blacks went in the side door and straight up the stairs," said Archie.

There was also a drive-in theater in the nearby towns of Tupelo, Nettleton, and Okolona with separate parking for Blacks, though whites could park wherever they wanted. When Archie and his friends went to the drive-in, the white teenagers would sometimes mess with them, and they'd talk back, but no major trouble broke out, fortunately.

Archie also enjoyed starring in school plays from about sixth to tenth grade.

"Each spring, it was the responsibility of each grade level to present a play as a fundraiser. I was the main character about three times, and would have hundreds of lines to learn. We would practice the last class period of the day and I would also practice at home. My mother would make sure I didn't miss any lines. I don't recall the titles, but the plays were mostly comedies or musicals. I played a variety of roles including the role of a father and businessman."

"I liked acting because it took my mind off of what was going around me and allowed me to focus on the role I was playing. It allowed me to imagine that I was there. There were no acting classes, you just went with what you thought the character was. And there was no one to encourage you that you had talent to pursue a career in acting. Later in life, after his kids were born, Archie said he play-acted around the house. "It was a way to loosen them up." Who knows, maybe it also influenced his younger daughter to go into acting.

His mother always came to watch the performances, though his father didn't attend anything at the school. During Archie's varsity year, he played basketball, and though they won a few games, he admits that the team wasn't that great.

"Maybe I could have been good if I could stretch myself to about 5'11'," he laughs. "But Tupelo got most of the really good players. If there was a good player in Shannon, he'd get recruited and move out to Tupelo and play for them."

Other than sports and plays, Archie also enjoyed dancing. His high school didn't allow any dances because the principal was a preacher. Instead, Archie and his friends went to dances at a community center near the church in the Pine Grove community.

"My mother taught me to dance," gloated Archie. "She was a great dancer. As kids, we danced all the time. There was a radio station out of Houston, Mississippi, and the DJ was white and tried to sound as if he was Black. Most listeners thought he was Black because he played songs you could dance to.

His program came on when school was letting out and you could call in and make requests."

"Then there was Randy's Records WLAC in Nashville Tennessee that played our type of music at night, both gospel and the latest pop and blues hits. That's where we ordered our records from."

There were juke joints around Shannon, too, which were bars that catered mostly to Blacks during the Jim Crow era, where people danced but also drank and gambled.

"I didn't like juke joints," said Archie, "because I didn't like to be around anything rowdy. I was not very shy, but I was quiet, and I didn't like to get in no mess."

When Archie and his friends went around in groups, his tendency to remain quiet helped to keep him out of trouble.

"We were always aware of our environment and we were always cautious. At night especially, we had to be concerned about what we said or where we looked."

In 1955, a fourteen-year-old boy named Emmett Till was lynched in Money, Mississippi, by two white men, after a white woman accused Till of flirting with her.

At the time of Till's murder, Archie was thirteen years old, and he lived just two hours away from the place where Emmett Till was murdered. A shockwave rolled through the country, and his part of the South in particular, when Till's body was discovered. Another shockwave rolled through when Till's murderers were not brought to justice.

It was an early lesson about what it meant to be a Black boy, and what you could or could not risk when interacting with whites, especially white females.

"I knew to be extra cautious around white women because there was always the fear that they could holler rape," he said. More than sixty years later, in 2017, Carolyn Bryant Donham, the woman who set Till's gruesome death into motion, admitted that she had lied. This confirmed what Archie and other Blacks knew at the time: even a lie from a white person could become a death sentence for a Black boy.

"After what happened to Emmett Till, my mother used to tell me not to take rides from white girls, and be careful accepting rides from some white boys even if they offered. In the South in those years, the white man and the Black woman had a freedom that a Black teenage boy did not have."

Archie doesn't recall witnessing any racial violence firsthand, but knew firsthand about the violence that some of his cousins and family faced. He can close his eyes and still hear name-calling from whites in his mind. He also vividly remembers the racist rhetoric of a Mississippi politician who used the N-word in speeches and called Blacks "lazy as hound dogs." And once, when he was still an adolescent, a store owner tried to trip his father, but his father caught the man's leg and sent him tumbling. Since it was the white man that started the scuffle, the other white men who knew and respected Archie's father discouraged the store owner from taking any revenge.

"My father worked for the Dabs and the Clarkes, all big men in Shannon, bankers and doctors. They stood up for him," Archie says.

White families and Black families lived in houses on the same country roads in Shannon. As children, Archie and other Black children would play with white kids, visiting each other's houses and hanging out together. Larry Johnson, who was white, and Archie became lifelong friends.

The Black women babysat white children, and little white girls used to come over to visit with his mother and grandmother.

All of this stopped when the kids reached adolescence. Around age twelve or thirteen, kids stopped visiting each other's houses and the white girls stopped coming to Black women for nurturing—it was an unwritten rule.

"The civil rights movement didn't hit Shannon like it hit other places," says Archie. "During my childhood, there wasn't a lot to do there except the truck stop, where Blacks already worked; nothing much to integrate or keep segregated. When I left Shannon in 1963, the movement was just beginning there."

Archie recalls that once, he and his friends stopped at a restaurant in Tupelo one evening in the summer of 1964 to get something to eat, and the restaurant refused to serve them. They sat there for thirty or forty minutes, just waiting and talking, not making any trouble. The police weren't called; there was no disturbance to report. Eventually, Archie and his friends just left.

That said, Archie always knew he had to be careful. Law enforcement kept a close eye on him and his friends; he didn't know this until he was older.

"One night in 1961 or '62, my friends and I were out having fun and encountered some white guys who threatened to harm us by coming into our community. So, a group of young Blacks set up a barricade right off the highway and waited for them—but they never showed up."

"My childhood was a learning experience," Archie recalled. "I learned what America is really like: how you can play with a white boy until a certain age, then wonder why you can't go to school together or how he could have privileges I didn't have. I also learned to look men in the eye and not be ashamed of who I am."

Although some Black families owned their own land in Shannon, including cousins of Archie, there were no Black men or women in positions of power back then, no police officers or city council members or school board members. There has never been a Black mayor in Shannon, though today, many Black citizens are city council members.

"There were plenty of people worse off than we were," Archie recalls of his childhood. "Today, Black folks are doing a lot better down there. No one is farming unless they want to. They have jobs, some own land and parcels of land, like my brother."

DATING

Archie had "little crushes," as he calls them now, throughout his early teen-age years, but not until age fifteen did he have a girlfriend. Her name was Earlene, and though they never went on a proper date, they used to attend basketball games together, or sit on her family's front porch and talk. It was on the porch, in fact, where Archie stole his first kiss.

"I was a nice-looking young man and girls were always attracted to me. But I didn't date until high school, because to date you needed a car, and I didn't have one."

His second girlfriend, and his first serious love, was Minnie Blackman, now Minnie Armstrong. They were the same age, but Minnie was ahead of Archie in school, and determined to go to college, which Archie respected. Together, they went dancing or to the café to play the jukebox. Archie was a good dancer and knew how to do the bop. He loved Sam Cooke, and Minnie loved Benny King. Once, Archie tried to pick up Minnie at her mother's house in Tupelo to bring her back to stay with her grandmother in Shannon. He couldn't afford to buy a quart of oil to put in the family car and messed up the motor before he arrived to pick her up. He was forced to call his cousins to come get him.

"Minnie was my first love," says Archie. "Our grandparents, everyone at school—they all thought we'd get married. We broke each other's heart."

36

They became sexually intimate during their time together but drifted apart after she left for college. Years later, after they'd parted ways and both graduated college, Archie visited Minnie and noticed a ring on her finger. "'If you say, take it off, I'll take it off,' Minnie said to me, but I said, 'No, you keep it.' It was a blow to me because I still had strong feelings for her, but I knew soon she would be another man's wife. Back then, girls were told that if they weren't married by age twenty-four, they were doomed. After Minnie, I wasn't serious about anyone else until I moved north."

CHAPTER 4

Early Spiritual Life

.... "*With God all things are possible*" –Matthew 19:26

Mama Ollie, Archie's maternal grandmother, was unquestionably his family's matriarch. She was a woman of unshakable faith, an important figure in the church and a Sunday school teacher, more like a second mother than a grandmother to her many grandchildren.

Like her daughter, Ruby, Mama Ollie left school to get married after finishing eighth grade—an extraordinary feat in her day, when girls rarely made it that far in school. Ollie had yearned to go on to high school and become a teacher but her family wouldn't allow it. In Archie's memory, Mama Ollie never worked in white people's homes. There were no jobs for Black women other than cooking, washing, ironing, cleaning the homes of white people, and caring for their children, all of which paid very little. She worked constantly in her own home and helped with the farming.

Mama Ollie was the one who steeped Archie in faith and spirituality from the time he could walk and talk. She spoke to him all the time about the Bible, unveiling stories to help him understand life. It was her influence that inspired Archie to go read the Bible by himself when he wasn't busy with either babysitting or his chores.

"Papa Arch was the oldest of four children. He was born in Poplar, Mississippi, just South of Shannon. His mother was Ella Knowles and I don't know who his father was, since he never mentioned him. I loved my grandfather, but I looked up to Mama Ollie more than Papa Arch," said Archie. "Papa would at times take some of us grandkids fishing in the creek, where we were allowed to play in the shallow water floating on inner tubes. He also taught me how to farm by helping him plant the seeds in the truck patch, which was like a large garden where peas, butter beans, white potatoes, sweet potatoes, watermelons, sweet corn, and popcorn were planted. Back then, most of the food we ate was produced on the farm. Papa Arch was a church deacon and a mason, too, but I observed from a young age that what he said didn't always match what he did. He drank whiskey, for example, and did other things that struck me as ungodly."

Mama Ollie was the opposite. She was always humming a spiritual hymn as she moved about the house, cooking, cleaning, or just sitting on the porch. Her love for the Lord was always top priority, never in doubt. "She had an enormous, lasting influence on me starting at a young age. Her great passions were the Lord and her family, in that order. And she always encouraged my relationship with God."

Mama Ollie was born in February 1898 in Shannon, Mississippi. She was the oldest child of fourteen children between Mack and Ella Trice. Her grandfather and grandmother were freed ex-slaves named Sam Trice and Martha Trice. When Archie was small, she used to tell him stories about her life as a little girl, growing up to love God, how she learned to hold her head high and be proud of who she was and where she came from. "God made her who she was," says Archie.

"She had some great stories," said Archie. "I recall her telling the story about a girl who loved to dance, and one day as she danced before the mirror, she was drawn into the mirror and never seen again. She often told ghost stories about the troubled spirits of former slaves walking around in certain areas of the community."

"She would talk about how she saw a lady and a girl walking across a pasture -- ghosts. It was always people who had been killed during slavery or the Civil war, and these people would become ghosts in her stories. Down by the creek, where something bad happened, Mama would say: 'the spirit is still there and is disturbed, so be careful when you're down there.' I had to walk a couple nights by myself about four miles, and I would think about the ghost stories she told all the way home until I finally got to my house. I didn't overcome my fear of darkness until I was 16 or 17 years old."

Archie said he and Floyd Wren, a childhood friend walked about three miles one night to go to a café. Floyd had cousins across town not too far from the café and when it was time for them to go home, Floyd decided that he would spend the night with his cousins. Archie, who was still afraid of the dark pleaded with his friend to walk home with him, but Floyd was determined to spend the night with kinfolk. So Archie had to make the 3-mile trek back by himself.

"I had ghost stories in my head. When you left the cafe you could go straight down the highway across the railroad tracks to get to where I lived. Then off the highway was a gravel road to take me home. If you go through town by yourself, maybe someone would pick on you. So I took the highway. I walked facing the traffic so I could see the cars coming. I had to pass a graveyard and my heart was beating fast."

"It sounded like someone was walking behind me. When I got to the low place in the road, about a mile from home, I saw something that looked like a person and I heard a noise. I jumped a fence and heard the noise again. To my relief, it was just a cow. I said to myself, Now, all these years people have been using scare tactics to frighten people like me. Well no more! That's how I overcame my fear of walking at night."

"My dad told me a story about leaving Gus Johnsons' store one night. He had to walk down the highway past the cemetery, through some fences, before he got home. He said there was something about the size of a cat following him. Although he was carrying groceries he started running. When he got home he banged on the door to be let in, and swore there was a ghost chasing him. Gus said it was a big dog who had taken a liking to him."

Archie said there was no shortage of ghost stories coming up.

"I also remember Mama Ollie talking about her first husband, the father of her first child, Aunt Virgie. He was a horse trader who left home one morning and was never heard of again. She believed that he was killed by some white men who were in the same business. I only wish now that I'd recorded our conversations, because there's so much I don't remember."

There was no one else who encouraged Archie in his faith and his self-worth the way Big Mama Ollie did. When Archie was nine years old, during a period when his father was up north working on the railroads, and Archie and his family were living with Papa Arch and Mama Ollie, Archie had his first significant spiritual awakening.

Maybe it was because he'd had more time to absorb Mama Ollie's teachings on faith and the Bible, or maybe it was because at the age of nine he was finally old enough, in the context of the family's Baptist Church, to choose to accept Christ as Savior and be baptized in the name of the Father, Son, and the Holy Spirit.

Whatever the reason, Archie feels God thought he was ready to receive the awakening of His Spirit within him. It happened on the back porch of his grandparents' home, where he had gone before church one Sunday morning to take some time to himself.

The morning was hot and humid, with a very light breeze on the screened porch. Archie wasn't thinking about anything in particular at the time, but like many nine-year-olds, just letting his thoughts jump freely around while fidgeting in the chair. It was the morning before the revival, which began that Sunday evening. All children nine years and older who had not been baptized were expected to sit on the mourner's bench and listen to the preacher to call sinners to accept Jesus Christ as their Savior, but Archie didn't know that yet.

As he sat alone on the porch, an unfamiliar sense of peace and calm came over him, a holy feeling unlike anything he'd ever felt before. He let the feeling soak into his bones. It was the Holy Spirit, Archie believed, letting him know that it was time for him to come home to Jesus.

"I had never felt anything like it before. It felt like bliss, almost like I was in the presence of God. I knew that I had changed and was ready to commit my life to Christ even though I was only a kid," recalled Archie.

Not everyone believed that a child of nine was mature or responsible enough to make the choice to accept Jesus Christ into his heart. Some Christians believe that a child should be at least twelve before accepting that kind of lifelong responsibility. But in the Johnson Chapel Missionary Baptist Church, children between age nine and twelve were routinely offered the option of being baptized. Any child who had been to Sunday school and taught about Christ was old enough, they believed, to make his or her own decision, just as Jesus had made his decision at age twelve. Many children waited, but on this day in August of 1951, Archie felt sure that he was ready.

There has always been a controversy in the church surrounding the question of at what age a child can decide to join the church. Religious scholars call this the Age of Accountability.

The Bible does not give a specific age at which people are accountable for the knowledge of their sins and their decision to accept or reject Jesus

Christ as their Savior. Some theologians say salvation is God's work in a person's heart, so it doesn't require any particular age requirement to be saved. They believe faith is more than a decision; it is a gift from God. For that reason, children's understanding and accepting of Jesus is no different than adults, they claim.

A survey by the International Bible Society found that 83% of all Christians made their commitment to Jesus Christ between the ages of 4 and 14, when they were children or in their early youth. Today, Archie supports letting children join the church and be baptized whenever they determine for themselves that they're ready to give their lives to Christ.

Although the concept of Jesus and the news of the Gospel may seem abstract for a child and for many adults, too, to comprehend, Archie prefers to emphasize God's unending love for them, and explain to them the care and community that comes with membership in a Christian family. He believes the rest will come as their faith matures.

Archie believes the age of accountability is different for all children. He thinks it can be defined as the age at which a child is capable of knowing and understanding that they are a sinner, recognizing that they needed a Savior, understanding that Jesus Christ is Savior and Lord, and realizing that we are saved only by the grace of God and not by virtue of anything we can do.

"Only God knows what that age is for each individual child," says Archie.

Other religious leaders think that by the age of twelve, most children will have reached the age of accountability. In the older Jewish and African traditions, a boy became a man and entered adulthood at age 12. This is consistent with Jesus' age when his parents brought him to the temple and he was found in deep theological conversations with the teachers far beyond his age.

Clearly, Archie found his religious faith at a young age. The church had always been the place where he's felt most comfortable. He may not have known it at the time, but he began his relationship with God at the age of nine and nearly seventy years later, believes that giving his life to Christ was the best decision he has ever made.

So, Archie went to church that Sunday evening, along with his mother, siblings, and grandparents. Before they sat down, Archie confided in Mama Ollie that the time had come for him to join the church. So, his grandmother told him to go to the pew up front in the church and sit on the mourner's bench. This was where people who hadn't yet been saved (accepted Christ) sat if they were interested in being baptized, and this is where Archie sat that evening. As the preacher was preaching, Archie stood up during the worship service, and in his words, gave his life to Christ.

His Grandmother Ollie's teachings were the primary foundation for Archie's decision, but he'd always had a strong feeling for the church. He'd always been moved by the pastor's preaching. And he had always, even before age nine, known that there was something different about himself, something that made him quieter and more contemplative than other kids his age. When he and his siblings played church at home, he'd always been the one to play the role of the preacher.

"I believe the Lord led me to it, because the timing was His to determine," said Archie. "That evening during the revival, I found myself standing up, crying, stepping toward to the pulpit, and reaching for the preacher. I kept thinking, thank you Jesus, thank you Jesus."

And so, that following Sunday around 8:00 in the morning, Archie and his family, other candidates for baptism, and the other members of the congregation all gathered around a small pond nearby, and Archie was baptized.

"Baptism is a visceral reminder," said Archie, "to think before you act. It's a lifelong commitment to consider one's own behavior and whether it's in line with the values of God's teaching, and curtail that behavior if it's not."

Archie has always known that he's not a perfect person; he has temptation like anyone else, but after being baptized, he also knew that there were certain things he could no longer do, certain paths no longer available to him. He was a changed person.

"I felt my sins had been washed away and I could now make a fresh start," recalled Archie.

Which isn't to say he never slipped up or made mistakes. Once, when he was still young, he got into his Papa's snuff and made himself really sick. He and his friends often took fruit from orchards and watermelons from the fields. Yet, he never stole anything from a store, nor ever vandalized, unlike many of his peers. Being poor often tested his faith, though.

He did his best to obey the Commandments. One day, he ran into a comic bookstore before seeing a movie. Time passed and he realized he'd be late for the movie if he didn't hurry. He says he unintentionally took a comic book with him when he left. After the movie when he realized his mistake, he returned, paid for the comic book, and apologized to the store owner. Since the store owner knew him, he didn't give Archie a hard time and accepted his apology.

Archie worked throughout his childhood to stay true to the promise he'd made to God, because he'd been saved.

CHAPTER 5

Off To College

"Be strong and of a good courage, fear not, nor be afraid of them: for the LORD thy God, he it is that doth go with thee; he will not fail thee, nor forsake thee." —Deuteronomy 31:6

O ther than Mama Ollie's unwavering belief in him, Archie received little practical guidance in how to prepare for college. Maybe this was because his own parents had no experience with college. There were so few peers on the college track and no school resources to help guide kids like him, who dreamed big. Without a school counselor or college advisor, there was no one who told him how to prepare for the entrance exams or what grades he'd need to achieve if college was going to be an option for him.

Instead, it was expected that a boy like Archie, who wanted to get out of Shannon after high school, would join the military or find a job out of town. Despite the fact that he earned good grades and graduated with honors, Archie began to think that college was not a realistic option. His grades weren't the problem—money was the problem.

During the spring of his senior year, Archie rode down to Jackson State College (now Jackson State University) in Jackson, Mississippi, with Coach

Paul Shack and another student who was trying to earn a basketball scholarship there. Paul had graduated from Jackson State.

"I just went along for the ride, to get out of town for the day," Archie explained. "But then I fell in love with the campus."

College was still only a sliver of a possibility, but he'd caught the fever.

After he graduated from high school and knew that he wanted to go to Jackson State, he still had no idea of his next step and no visible path to college.

One night, he stopped by his Aunt Larabelle's house before going home after work. Aunt Larabelle was his grandmother's sister-in-law. For a while, he just sat on her front porch swing, watching cars pass by on the road in front of the house.

After a while, Aunt Larabelle came to the door and asked him what he was doing.

"Just sitting here thinking," he told her.

"You're thinking about going to college, aren't you?" Larabelle stated in her calm steady voice.

Archie was surprised. Getting out of Shannon and going to college was exactly what had been on his mind, not only that moment but all of the time since he had visited the campus. He was a twenty-year-old man just out of high school, and he had no clear plans for the next stage of his life. College was still a pipe dream.

"Yes, but I can't afford it," he told her. "Maybe I'll join the military." He hadn't breathed a word to a soul, but he'd started to think he might join the military that July.

"If you want to go to college, I'll help you," Aunt Larabelle promised. "I'll pay your first quarter's tuition."

When Archie remembers this moment, even all these years later, he still finds himself getting emotional. Had he gone to his aunt's house that day looking for divine intervention? Because that's what her offer felt like to him. His prayer had been answered.

Though she was the first person to clear a path for him, Aunt Larabelle wasn't the first to believe that Archie could go to college. Mrs. Iola Henderson, Archie's fifth grade teacher, had also told him he was college material. But it was Aunt Larabelle's financial assistance that made it possible.

Before he could take Larabelle up on her offer, he needed to get admitted. He had to take the college entrance exams. He rode three hours with Grace Trice, a high school classmate, and her father to take the test. He performed well enough to be admitted to Jackson State. Over the summer, while doing carpentry work, he fortuitously met Jimmie Trimble, who was also headed to Jackson State. This would be the beginning of a lifelong friendship.

Archie credits divine providence when asked about meeting Jimmie. He lived in Tupelo, Mississippi, had recently graduated from Carver High School, which was the colored high school there. "We met in Pete's Barber Shop where Jimmie and I went to get haircuts. I learned from Pete that Jimmie Trimble would be attending Jackson State in the fall. One day after work, Jimmie stopped by the barber shop and Pete introduced us. We exchanged contact information and agreed to become roommates once we arrived on campus. We discovered we had a lot in common. We both came from large families, were Christians, enjoyed many of the same things, and were around the same age."

That fall, the weekend before college started, Archie took a Trailways bus down to Jackson State on a Saturday. Since the dormitory didn't open up until the next day, Archie slept in the bus station that night. He was up bright and early on Sunday and was one of the first in line when they opened the dorm doors. Also waiting was Jimmie Trimble.

"We got a room together in Stewart Hall. We became like brothers and were roommates throughout our college years, sharing our food, our clothes, and what little funds we were blessed to earn."

Although Aunt Larabelle had paid his first quarter's tuition, Archie knew he would need to find a job to be able to stay in school. The very next day, he set out to find work on campus. By Tuesday, Archie had found employment in the maintenance department of Jackson State. Mr. J. Y. Woodard helped him get the job by speaking with Mr. Cunningham who was the Supervisor of building and grounds. He started off doing repair work between classes. He worked twenty hours a week and made just enough for room and board, not a penny extra.

For spending money, Archie took on odd jobs like hanging curtains or working on lawns, and he sold his own blood every six weeks.

"You can still see the mark on my arm," he said. "It paid just enough for me to have a little change in my pocket. My mother would send me a few dollars once in a while. I found out after college that she borrowed the money she sent me. I guess that's why I place such a high value on what I've accomplished to this day, because of all the sacrifices my family and I made, especially my mother."

When Archie wasn't in class, he was at work. At night, he studied in the library or in his dorm room.

Archie was determined, even in college, to make up the difference he perceived between himself and his peers, resulting from being held back in grade school.

Archie's parents were proud that their oldest graduated high school and made it to college. His father finally acknowledged it, to Archie's surprise. One weekend, when Archie was home from college, his mother sent him down to the grain elevator to pick up his father's paycheck.

"I remember my father standing there telling people, including a white man, 'That's my boy, he's in college.' I could tell he was proud. He never said he loved me, but that moment told me he did."

Archie was truly grateful to be in college, but working to pay for it took every minute of free time. He'd wanted to try out for the baseball team but couldn't because of work.

"There was a Black Student Union, too, but with my work hours, I didn't even have time to join or even pledge a fraternity," says Archie. "On some weekends, I might get away long enough to share a pitcher of beer with my friends, Jimmie Trimble and Willie Woods, or play intramural softball."

Archie chose Industrial Education as his major because he wanted to be a mechanical engineer, and that was the closest thing Jackson State offered. If there had been some kind of college advising available before he graduated from high school, he believes he might have gone to a school with a stronger engineering program.

J. Y. Woodard, who became like a father figure to those majoring in Industrial Education, was head of the Department of Industrial Education. After Archie's first quarter, during which he was working all hours and struggling to get his bearings, Woodard looked at Archie's first quarter grades and said to him, "You're wasting your parents' money."

This was just the kick in the pants Archie needed to get focused. Archie vowed to prove to Mr. Woodard that he was a serious student and his grades improved for the rest of his college tenure.

Other influential teachers were Dr. Jefferson in the Humanities department and Dr. McAlister in Psychology. Both taught Archie things like critical thinking and how to reason effectively.

Archie became a role model to younger kids in Shannon merely by attending college, something very few young people from Shannon had done. His success encouraged most of his own siblings to graduate from high school, except for Ollie, who earned her GED years later.

"In my community, there were only two other kids around my age who went to college. People were proud of me," recalled Archie.

Archie wasn't much of a party-goer during college, or after. There was a Christian organization on campus, but he never got involved. Instead, from time to time, he went off-campus to a local church for service and Sunday school. He also attended Vesper Services on most Wednesdays at noon.

Every so often, he and friends would take up a booth at a local bar called Cooper's Place or the College Inn. "We bought one pitcher of beer and sipped as slowly as we could, because as long as it wasn't empty, they couldn't kick us out," Archie recalled.

When he could manage it, Archie would save money so he could make it to a show or two off campus, at a music club called the Elks Club. Tickets were only $1.50 back then. Over the years, he saw performances there by Tina Turner, James Brown, BB King, and other rising Black stars.

Archie's job in the maintenance department was a mainstay of his college career. He worked for a man named Mr. Taylor, who took a liking to Archie and assigned Mr. Bennett as his work partner.

"Bennett was a little short guy who smoked a pipe and wore white overalls," Archie recalls of his colleague. "Bennett taught me tricks of the trade and carpentry, and brought me along on jobs all over campus. As a maintenance worker, I was allowed to go places other students couldn't go, like the President's house and the Dean's house—and even the girls' dormitory." When he had work at the girls' dorm, he'd have to holler "Man in the hall!" as he moved through the building, just in case a girl was walking out of the shower.

Once, Archie and Bennett were in the auditorium in the language arts department, and Archie had to climb a thirty-two-foot ladder to do a repair.

"When I got to the top, it started to slide down," he recalls. "Just before it hit the floor, I jumped off. That experience taught me how God can protect you, because I don't know how I walked away without getting hurt." Bennett told him at the time that he must have been wearing his lucky charm.

This wasn't the only time during college when Archie felt like someone was looking out for him. He was playing intramural baseball in the outfield and had an experience he recalls clearly more than fifty years later.

"Visualize this," he said. "There was an old cistern well out in the field, where you dropped down a bucket on a rope, and around it was a concrete wall, about knee-high. I was running to catch a fly ball and took my eyes off the field. I hit that cistern wall right at my knee and it flipped me clean over."

The accident fractured his knee cap. He was laid up for a couple of weeks and had to use crutches.

"That could have been a lot worse. I didn't think it at the time but now I wonder if maybe I was already under the Lord's protection."

Through his job working in the maintenance department, he got to know all the people in the dining hall, too. They teased him because his hands were always dirty, but Archie held his head high and felt the job was a highlight of his college experience. "I was proud of making it through in four years, and I was proud of how I carried myself. Despite the odds, I made it through."

At Jackson State, Archie received a well-rounded education. In his position in the maintenance department, he not only learned a trade, but he also learned how to apply his college experience to the real world.

"Learning isn't just about the textbook—it's about relating to people and applying the tricks of the trade you can only learn in real life."

Jackson State was, almost from the outset, a nurturing experience for Archie. He was surrounded by kids from bigger cities with parents who were better educated, but after the first semester his grades improved considerably.

During his first college summer, he worked at the Agricultural Department of Lee County, surveying farm fields, by marking off the acres used for farming. He recalls, "I had completed one year of college and was paired with a white boy just out of high school. He had the note pad, plotting the numbers, and I was labeled the 'chain boy doing the manual labor.' It seemed like nothing much had changed in Mississippi."

PROTEST

Lynch Street ran right through the center of the Jackson State campus, and students crossed that street several times a day to get to their classes and to the dining hall. In the evenings, traffic could be heavy. Student groups had been asking the administration for a streetlamp and a stop sign so crossing would be safer, but none had been installed. One evening, a female student was struck by a car and broke her leg trying to cross the street.

This led to a series of protests that turned violent when some athletes started throwing rocks and bricks at passing cars as they drove through campus. The tension was high because it was the time of the Freedom Riders, and the early stages of the civil rights movement. The campus erupted and Allen C. Thompson, the mayor of Jackson, ordered the National Guard to put down the unrest. The next thing students knew, they were surrounded by Jeeps full of guards holding M16 rifles. After that, there was a curfew.

"I never threw a rock, but I participated in the protests. Still, it was all new to me."

At least this protest wasn't fatal like the one three years later on May 15, 1970, widely known as the Jackson State Massacre. Students had gathered on Lynch Street to protest what turned out to be a false rumor—the death of Civil Rights Activist, Charles Evers, the older brother of Medgar Evers who was assassinated in 1963.

Black students allegedly pelted rocks at white motorists driving down the main road of campus. Lynch Street was frequently the site of confrontations between Black and White residents and this false rumor just added to the tension. When fires were started and vehicles overturned, the firefighters who were dispatched to the scene called in the police.

The police responded in full force with over seventy-five Jackson police officers along with the Mississippi Highway Patrol arriving on campus. When the police moved in to control the crowd in the early morning hours, they claimed a sniper was on one of the upper floors of the dorm and was firing at them so they started shooting.

The crowd scattered and two students, Phillip Lafayette Gibbs, 21, a junior at Jackson State, and James Earl Green, 17, a senior at nearby Jim Hill High School, were killed; twelve others were wounded. Gibbs was killed near Alexander Hall by buckshot, while Green was killed behind the police line in front of B. F. Roberts Hall, also with a shotgun.

The students say they did not provoke the officers. More than 460 shots were fired by patrolman using shotguns from thirty to fifty feet away. Every window of the building facing Lynch Street was shattered.

The President's Commission on Campus Unrest investigated the killings and concluded that the police's action was an "unreasonable, unjustified overreaction" and that there was no sniper fire. Still, there were no arrests in connection with the deaths at Jackson State.

Jackson State has now memorialized the event by naming the area in which the killings occurred, Gibbs-Green Plaza. A large stone monument in front of Alexander Hall also honors the victims. The tragic event is shared with new students during orientation and taught in some liberal arts classes so that what happened on campus over fifty years ago will never be forgotten.

That summer, after the initial protest resulting from the female student getting injured, Archie returned home and his father told him something that made his blood run cold.

"Be careful," said his father, "because you're being watched."

The FBI was watching Black Americans involved in the civil rights movement at all levels. Local sheriffs and cops in Mississippi were doing the same. While Archie was aware of the civil rights movement, his work and class schedules didn't allow him to become actively involved. He felt if they were watching someone like him, then things had become more sinister than he thought in this country. "I supported the civil rights struggle but I wasn't even a minor player."

Archie graduated in the spring of 1967. It took him four years plus one summer, but he did it. Three family members attended the ceremony: his mother and Hosea and Lavelle Foster.

"My mother was proud, and told me so. She said that the Lord will show you the way although you might need to put in some work. I was ready to begin a new chapter in my life. I had my degree. I had just been offered a new job and I was ready to go face the world. All right, God, lead the way!"

CHAPTER SIX
The Move North

*"Have not I commanded thee? Be strong and of a good courage;
be not afraid, neither be thou dismayed: for the Lord thy
God is with thee whithersoever thou goest."* —Joshua 1:9

During Archie's last semester at college, Milwaukee Public School Recruiters visited Jackson State seeking talented and enthusiastic teachers for their school system that was becoming increasingly Black. When Archie and his roommate, Jimmie Tremble, heard of the opportunity, they, like several other Jackson State students, jumped at the chance to leave the South and both signed a contract a few months before graduating from college. It was 1967, and he'd be paid an annual salary of $5850. "I felt great about that," said Archie. "It was a new beginning."

"I was drafted after I graduated college. I arrived in Milwaukee in August and was drafted in September. I applied for a deferment with the Milwaukee draft board. Because I'd elected to teach in an inner city school, I got an occupational deferment, which I renewed each year. In college I had to keep my grades above a 2.5 average to stay out of the military. If the grades fell, they'd pull you out. With this deferment I could now pursue my teaching career."

Archie was ready to get out of the South, which was the only place he'd known up to that point. Milwaukee wasn't only a bigger city, it was the North, and held all the mystery and promise of a foreign land.

Archie held certain assumptions before leaving the South. The North was considered more progressive and less segregated, for example. In terms of jobs, there was rumored to be much more opportunity, because in Mississippi, there were almost no jobs for Blacks with college degrees. Not everyone could go into teaching after all, and the pay in rural southern areas was next to nothing. Besides, Mississippi schools were still segregated when Archie left and he was curious about what it would be like to teach in an integrated school.

"I went where the opportunity was," Archie emphatically stated.

With the money he'd earned over the summer, he bought a bus ticket, and when he and Jimmie arrived in Milwaukee, they walked from the bus station to the house of Ella Parnell, Hosea Foster's aunt, whom Archie had called about a room before leaving Mississippi.

"I barely had enough money to pay room and board for a month," recalls Archie.

The following day, he and Jimmie reported to orientation at the central office of the Milwaukee Public Schools. There, they met Earnest Lockhart, another Jackson State graduate, whose sister had a room to rent in her home on 17th street. After that first week with the Parnells, Archie and Jimmie moved into Olivia Lee's home, where they continued to live until the following January.

The summer of 1967 was a memorable one in United States history, especially for Blacks living in larger cities and on the front lines of the civil rights movement. That summer, which is known forever as the Long Hot Summer of 1967, brought about 159 protests and outbursts in cities across the nation. One of those cities was Milwaukee, Wisconsin.

In Milwaukee, the unrest had its roots in Black discontent resulting from housing discrimination and police brutality. The actual outburst is alleged to have started with how the police handled a fight between teenagers, and instead of calming the situation, escalated it to a full-scale disturbance. Blacks had more than enough and took their frustration to the streets. The mayor instituted a curfew and brought in the National Guard at the end of July.

During the disturbance, at least three Blacks were killed as well as one police officer. There were over a hundred injured, 1740 arrests, and thousands of dollars of damage to businesses. Although the curfew was lifted in the first week of August, tensions remained high, and Black and white residents continued to clash over housing demonstrations throughout the month.

On August 27th, the local NAACP, and local priest and activist, Father James Groppi, held an equal-housing march into a white neighborhood and were met with stoning, thrown garbage, and racial slurs. According to news articles, two days later, Groppi led another march, this time toward Kosciuszko Park, a primarily white neighborhood, where a mob of 13,000 met them with sniper fire and drove them back to their headquarters, which was burned down later that night.

Groppi and many others were arrested. Reverend Dr. Martin Luther King, Jr., sent a telegram from Atlanta in support of Milwaukee's "courageous leaders," who had advocated and organized nonviolent protests. King said they were "demonstrating that it is possible to be militant and powerful without destroying life or property."

Although Archie did not participate in the protests, he was well aware of them as he began his new career up north. He thought he would escape the overt racism he encountered in the South, but soon discovered that Jim Crow had made the trip north with him. The housing discrimination Blacks faced in Milwaukee was proof that racism was still very much alive even on this side of the Mason-Dixon Line.

In fact, he thought it was almost as bad as in the South, if not worse in some ways. Because of redlining, Blacks all lived in the same neighborhoods, so some schools were primarily white and others primarily Black, including the one where Archie was assigned, Robert Fulton Middle School.

"At least in the South, we knew where we stood," said Archie. "We knew where the lines were. The whites would say, 'The law says we've got to do this, so we'll do it.' And in the South, I knew how to stay safe."

But the North was a whole new world. The housing pattern alone was confusing: in the rural South, homes had been spread out, with Blacks and whites living on the same country roads, but in the North, all the houses and buildings were clustered together, with Blacks in one place and whites everywhere else. And many people in Milwaukee were even poorer than Archie's family down South. Many city dwellers were doing housework and other low-paying jobs just to scrape by.

He realized that when he was growing up in Shannon and relatives from the North came to visit, they had disguised their poverty out of pride. So, it took him some time to adjust to this new reality.

But despite the city's segregation and poverty, Archie couldn't help but find Milwaukee alluring and exciting. There were so many things to see and do; so many restaurants and neighborhoods to visit. He was in awe of the architecture, great music, new smells, and foreign languages spilling out into the streets. He also found the city initially welcoming, because of people like the Parnells and Olivia Lee who had opened their homes to him and Jimmie.

Ms. Lee liked both Archie and Jimmie and allowed them to drive her car to get groceries and run errands. Archie, promising himself to become independent, soon familiarized himself with the Milwaukee bus system, and then carpooled with another teacher from the school, Willie Killins, who coincidently also graduated from Jackson State.

"What I found in Milwaukee when I arrived was a city where Black people respected each other and offered the same kind of hospitality they'd offered back home, where extended families connected, and people helped each other out until they could stand on their own," said Archie. "People don't do that for each other today."

"Most of the Black folks in Milwaukee at that time had come from the South, like me," said Archie. He'd expected everything to be new in Milwaukee but since he found a temporary home among his own kin, his transition was smooth. They fed him the same food he'd eaten at home, grits for breakfast, or he'd get breakfast at Third and Center streets at a restaurant before work, including eggs, gravy, and biscuits.

Worship services were similar as well, especially in Baptist churches. The Blacks who had migrated north had brought along the same church organization and structure they'd practiced in the South. "The gospel music, the choirs, the preaching, it was all familiar."

Still, many of Archie's expectations of the North did not pan out, which was a profound disappointment. In the South, he'd understood where he and his family stood in the larger community, and in the rural areas, outside of Shannon proper. Blacks and whites had lived on adjoining lots. They knew each other, and they knew their places.

In Milwaukee, neighborhoods were segregated by race, and though white people at his school seemed to accept him as an equal, after he scratched the surface, it would be apparent that they still considered themselves more intelligent and superior. Blacks and whites might work in the same jobs, but the whites still earned more.

In November of 1967, three months after arriving in Milwaukee, Archie finally bought himself a car. Owning his first car, a 1967 Buick Grand Sport

400, was a dream come true, and gave him a certain degree of independence, freedom, and accomplishment he'd always felt he lacked. The car was a symbol of the success he'd made for himself, not only by moving to a city where he only knew a handful of people but trusting in his faith that he was in the city where he was supposed to be. He didn't know what challenges lay ahead but he was ready to find out.

CHAPTER SEVEN
Working In Milwaukee's Schools

"For with God nothing shall be impossible" —Luke 1:37

Archie's first position in the Milwaukee Public Schools was to teach at Robert Fulton Middle School located at 2760 N. 1st Street. At Robert Fulton, where Archie stayed until 1975, he taught sixth and seventh graders woodshop, metal shop, drafting, electric shop, and math.

Fulton itself was a place wrought with institutional challenges, and kids of color living in poverty composed most of the student population. The teachers, Archie included, called it "Blackboard Jungle" after the movie with Sidney Poitier.

"I spent nine years in that school," says Archie, "and I don't regret a day."

When he arrived, Fulton's principal and vice principal were both white men. There was one Black staff member who dealt mostly with discipline issues, and had no authority to make major decisions. When Archie looked around his classroom, he saw that this was a population of kids who had been forgotten by the system, who were being left behind every day. He knew he had a tremendous challenge on his hands to teach what the system called neglected, angry, and chaotic students, but he also saw the opportunity to make change. In his heart, he felt like he could be facing a younger version of himself if fate had dealt him a slightly different hand.

"I learned during those years that those kids needed someone who cared about them. I did for them what some of my teachers did for me, especially Mrs. Henderson. I took them under my wing and insisted that they learn," Archie declared. Despite the fact that Fulton would turn out to be a good fit for him, Archie's early days at the school were an exercise in frustration. He struggled to break through the barriers that so many kids had created as a means of survival, which was often reflected by their inattentive and boisterous behaviors.

"Within the first year, I had made up my mind to quit," he recalled. But then the chair of his department, a man named Duncan Galloway, who was an Honorary Tuskegee Airman and served in the Airforce during WWII, gave him some good advice about teaching sixth and seventh graders. Galloway told Archie that despite the rough reputation of the school at large, that the class he had been assigned was in fact a pretty good group. Archie didn't see it that way. All he saw were endless discipline problems.

Galloway then told him to forget about teaching by the book, to throw away the textbook curriculum and find a new way to do it. His own way. Doing things his own way had always been Archie's preference but he had always hesitated. He didn't want to rock the boat. But now he had been given the green light, so that's what he did.

Archie had an advantage that many other teachers and administrators at Fulton didn't. He'd been born and raised in poverty, too, like so many of his students. He also knew how it felt to be dismissed and held back and underestimated by grownups and peers.

"I realized I needed to show the kids that I could identify with them. My upbringing enormously helped me to do that," he said.

In 1971, Archie's father passed away at the young age of 53, just after Reggie (Archie's first son) was born. After his father's death, Archie was thinking about something his father had said to him once when he was a boy. He'd been frustrated that he had to go work in the field instead of playing baseball with his friends, and his father had said to him, "Son, you have your hand in the lion's mouth. You must work easy until you get it out."

The words haunted Archie, and one day when they were sitting together, he asked Galloway what he thought his father meant.

"Galloway said he thought my father was trying to teach me to be patient. When you're in a difficult situation, have patience until you can get yourself out of it," he said.

Galloway became a mentor to Archie. When he left his position to go into full-time guidance counseling, Archie became the department chair. Archie proved that he was good at building relationships with the kids, at listening to them, and getting through to them.

"Rebellious kids aren't rebelling because they don't like school," Archie explained. "They're rebelling because of where they come from. One year, there was a young man in my class who wouldn't read when I called on him in class. Eventually, I discovered he didn't know how, so I gave him out-of-class assignments that would help him read." Archie remembered fondly the cardboard alphabet which his mother created with shoe polish-drawn letters to help him learn to read. He felt freed by Dean Galloway to use different creative approaches with the individual students.

During the late 1960s and early '70s, Fulton earned a reputation in Milwaukee for its unruly student body. Fights often broke out after school, and the local media would show up to cover the violence, which meant that the city was getting a very negative image of what the school was all about, since fighting was far from the whole picture.

In 1968, Mr. John Davis from Louisiana, who was serving as Principal at Palmer Elementary school, was reassigned to be Principal at Fulton. John began a process of building better relationships between staff, teachers, and students to foster community pride in the school. The home economics, industrial education, and art departments came together to plan their first school-wide exhibition to display the students' work. They invited the media two weeks in advance, but no media showed up.

"They weren't interested in something positive about the school, just the negative," Archie alleged.

When Archie reflects on his time in the school system, he feels proud of the impact he made in the lives of the children he taught and led. He recalls that the only white kid in one of his classes got picked on by his classmates. Archie defended him, and years later the boy became a locksmith. Archie occasionally runs into him around town.

"He told me he would never forget what I did for him," recalls Archie.

The kids he knew all those years ago when he was teaching at Fulton are now adults, many of whom still live and work in Milwaukee. The current sheriff of Milwaukee County was one of Archie's seventh graders. When Archie runs into former students, they still remember the positive impression he made on them.

"They remember me as a great teacher," explains Archie. "That's a beautiful thing."

During his 23 years in Milwaukee Public Schools, Archie worked at four different schools in total. In two, he was a teacher, and in the others, he worked in the administration. During his years at Milwaukee Tech—now Bradley Tech—he continued to hone his skills relating to young people and getting through to them. Still, it was at Milwaukee Tech where he says he faced the most racism.

Archie says he received a cool reception by fellow teachers in the department. "They shared curriculum materials and lesson plans, while I had to make my own. There was one fellow teacher in particular who came into my classroom and walked around observing as if he was my immediate supervisor," Archie states. "After our conversation about this, he never came into my classroom again in that manner. For three years, I taught five drafting classes in three different classrooms, on two floors. The classrooms would have locked closets and desks."

"The first year I was there, a white student contested the grade he received on an assignment. He told me that he was bringing his father in to discuss the matter because he had taken drafting as a student at Tech. Like I didn't know what I was doing. I had to constantly deal with racism and the micro-aggressions that Black teachers still endure."

Despite the racism he faced, Archie thinks he was able to make an impact, mostly because he followed his own lead and was always firm and fair, and put a lot of kids on the right track during his tenure there.

"My moral grounding served me well in school, along with my Mama Ollie's principle, which was to treat every living being with respect. But I still felt there was something empty inside of me. Something was missing. I just wasn't doing enough with my life," he quietly confessed.

He stayed in the classroom as long as he did because of the success of his style of relating to the kids; he could always see how he was doing good. By then, a colleague at Tech noticed how much guidance he offered teachers and administrators. Janie Hatton who was an assistant principal, mentioned to Archie that he would be a good fit for an assistant principal or principal role. Archie gave it some serious consideration and eventually decided to pursue administrative work. He felt he could have an even greater impact on the lives of the students as an administrator. Teachers work with select groups; administrators work with everyone in the school.

As an administrator, Archie said he was still able to make a difference. He dressed professionally and modeled professionalism, and yet, he says he often stepped into the vital role of a trusted adult.

"I would tell the young people, when they leave home and get on the bus, they become my responsibility. And they keep being my responsibility until they're back home safely," he said.

For the most part, the populations of his schools were mostly Black and Hispanic. At South Division High School where he was Assistant Principal, Archie says the school was full of kids who were in Hispanic or Black gangs.

Archie recalls a day when he needed to discipline a Hispanic student, and the young man's grandfather came to school to vouch for him. Archie noticed a Latin King gang tattoo on the older man's hand. "For a lot of kids, Black and Hispanic, multiple generations were involved in gangs. That's how they believed they could survive. I still communicated with them and related to them, and we didn't allow anything from outside of school to happen within the school's walls. There were no ill feelings when I disciplined them, because gang or not, I showed respect and demanded it," said Archie.

And much of the same story played out at each new school. He had been the principal at North Division high school for two years before he felt he'd truly earned the trust of his staff and colleagues. That school was—in his words—a dumping ground for kids with poor behavior. It was an uphill battle to prove to the students that they were safe at school, and that it was a place of learning, not chaos. So, he put stricter guidelines in place, such as being prompt and on time to school and class, instituted a dress code, prohibited electronic devices (back then, pagers and cell phones), required the use of proper language in classrooms, banned weapons on school premises, as well as requiring see-through backpacks. Furthermore, he prohibited street gang representation on school premises, and asked all students to show respect for self and others. Some of the teachers figured the students would just stop coming to school. But they didn't, and as a result, he made inroads with the student population.

In his early days at North Division, he felt like a figurehead with no real value or power. One day, the head of the union took over Archie's closed-door meeting. Archie simply got up and walked out. Later, the union official admitted that the teachers who remained at the meeting had eaten him alive with questions and criticisms and denounced his arrogance for disrupting the meeting.

"That's when I knew I had the teachers on my side," recalls Archie.

The same thing happened at a parent group meeting, with a school board member who tried to dictate policy. The parent group rose up, defended their principal and boldly told the board member that they wouldn't let him undercut Archie's administration.

"That's when I knew I had the parents, too."

He was beginning to get the results and have the impact he wanted.

"If you involve people and give them ownership, if you're not a dictator, teamwork works. This is true in ministry as well."

Though he was welcome to stay on, he retired four years after becoming a North Division's Principal. He still had that feeling inside himself that there was more he was called to do.

Today Archie believes schools in urban centers like Milwaukee have undergone a sea change.

"There used to be kids who came to school just for auto shop, metal shop, wood shop, electric shop, consumer education, music and art. They left school with life skills and soft skills and they went away prepared for life. Now, they don't prepare kids for life. There's so much bad language and disrespect and wandering the halls—schools are out of control. And they've given so many rights to the kids and taken away rights from the teachers. Their hands are tied," Archie sadly admitted.

The answer, Archie believes, is to get good teachers and pay them well. Wisconsin's teachers are woefully underpaid, he believes partly because of Republican former Governor Scott Walker's Act 10, and partly because of laws that permit private schools to be subsidized with public money.

While Archie sits on a board that gives Black students school choice, he defends his actions by stating that's what school choice was originally intended to do. According to Archie it was meant to be used only for under-privileged kids. "Instead, what's happening everywhere," said Archie, "is that white people are using the programs for themselves, setting up their own private schools and taking public funds.

The underlying problems in failing schools," argues Archie, "is racism. Teachers treat Black kids and white kids differently at every level. A Black kid acting out might get put on Ritalin or be suspended. A white kid is told he's bored. No one is telling kids that they aren't misfits, that there are skills they can learn in school to prepare them for a life they will want."

Archie experiences this firsthand because he serves as a hearing officer for Milwaukee Public Schools, helping to decide students' verdicts in expulsion hearings. The behaviors he is witnessing is as bad as any Archie has ever witnessed during his tenure in the school district. When he intervenes, he asks both boys and girls, "Do you like yourself?"

One boy replied that no, he didn't.

"Why?" asked Archie.

"Because," said the boy.

Archie pressed him. "Because why? Who defines you?"

Archie said he uses this opportunity to counsel young people on how to start liking themselves and to start making better decisions about their lives.

He encourages them to get focused and concentrate on what they need out of their school experience.

In many cases, the parents are struggling too, Archie believes.

"We have so many young parents who don't know how to parent. I remember one time a mother called in crying because she couldn't get her ninth grader out of bed to get to school. I told her, 'That's your house and your child. You get him here and I'll help him once he gets here,'" Archie said.

Sadly, Archie's experience tells him that the Milwaukee schools, like many other urban centers in the country, have only gotten worse over the years.

"I could not function in the school system today," he said. "Back then, I said a little prayer every morning to get through the day. Now, I would be praying non-stop."

CHAPTER EIGHT

First Lady And Family

"He that loveth not knoweth not God;
for God is love." –1 John 4:8

W hile still in high school, prior to leaving for Jackson State, Archie made a date with a high school classmate whom he'd known for years, a girl who lived in the next township. They planned to go to the movies, but on the night of their date, Archie's mother's car wouldn't start. He ran to his uncle's house to use the phone, to call her and apologize. Their date would have to wait.

Archie was disappointed. It was another moment from his teenage years when his fate was determined by his lack of personal transportation, a fact that dogged him for years.

Archie and his former classmate didn't set another date right away. They bumped into each other every now and then at the Smith Dairy Bar when Archie was home on visits from college. Meanwhile, Archie had other girl-friends, including Minnie Blackmon, who went to Alcorn State, another historically Black college in Mississippi.

When he was a junior at Jackson State, Archie visited Alcorn for a football game, planning to rendezvous with Minnie. Instead, he ran into his old friend from high school, the girl from the movie date that never happened. It had been three years but they ended up laughing and talking for hours together and then he walked her back to her dorm room.

"We didn't kiss that night," recalled Archie. "But there was always something in the back of my mind, something tenderly holding a place there for her."

A few months after Archie graduated from college and moved to Milwaukee in 1967, his roommate Jimmie Trimble, who had also come to Milwaukee to teach, ran into the girl at the Brothers Jazz Lounge. She was with her brother, Medford, whom Archie knew from high school and who had stayed with Archie and Jimmie a couple days as he passed through Jackson visiting a friend. Medford had been in the Army during college, and unbeknownst to Archie, had moved to Milwaukee after his honorable discharge.

Medford gave Jimmie his number and asked him to tell Archie to call. Archie called the very next day, and lo and behold, who answered the phone but the girl he had made a date with while she was a senior in high school. The same young woman he had walked to the dorm when she was a freshman at Alcorn State, who would later become his wife, Jeanette Rogers. Archie hadn't even known she was living in the same town.

"On that first phone call, I asked if we could go out, and here we are fifty years later," smiles Archie.

For their first official date, they went to a jazz club. They instantly connected on a personal level and made it a priority to see each other every two or three days.

"We had a connection-something special. I'd never had much of a prob-lem with girls, but I'd never felt the way I did with Jeanette. By the third time we went out, I knew."

So, on just their third date, he put all his cards on the table. That very night they had the kind of honest conversation that would serve them throughout their fifty-plus years together. He revealed that what he felt was more than attraction, that he was serious, and that he could see a future with her.

This was in February of 1968, and on Christmas Eve of the same year, he proposed.

"My proposal wasn't on one knee, but I had a ring and I knew it was the right size. I picked it out myself and wrapped it in a box that was larger than the ring box. We were at my apartment, and I told her I had something for her. When she finally found the ring, I asked if I could put it on her finger, and she said 'yes'."

They were married on September 27, 1969, at her brother's house, followed by a reception at the YMCA. Jeanette, a talented seamstress, made her own wedding gown. Jimmie Trimble was Archie's best man and Jeanette's maid of honor was her oldest sister, Mattie. There was no honeymoon because the young couple couldn't afford one. In fact, by the time they took their first real vacation together, they already had two of their three children.

Jeanette was born in 1947, being five years younger than Archie. She was the youngest of five children, three brothers and one sister. When she was only four years old her father died of pneumonia. He'd been hunting in the wintertime with a group of white men who paid him to find coons and flush them out. There was no reliable medical care for Black men like Jeanette's father, so he died of an illness that many white men were routinely treated for and successfully recovered.

Jeanette also grew up in Shannon, in the Good Hope community. Her family worshiped at the Good Hope Missionary Baptist Church, whereas Archie's family was in the Johnson Chapel Missionary Baptist Church community. Jeanette's mother was Lee Rene Rogers, and her grandmother was Lucy Knowles, although Jeanette called her Mama Lucy. Mama Ida, a woman Jeanette recalls as particularly stingy with treats, was Jeanette's paternal grandmother, and her grandfather was a religious man named John Rogers.

"It was a simple life," Jeanette explains. "We grew all our vegetables and raised our animals. We had cows, Clydesdales, a pony named Ben, and two mules for farming. There were no tractors." Jeanette inherited her father's love of the outdoors.

"I picked cotton, chopped cotton and weeded. I didn't like farming but I did love being outside."

After Jeanette's father died, the family received welfare assistance. Her mother never remarried. Jeanette still recalls visits from the social worker, who snooped around their house on the hunt for "luxury items," which would disqualify the family from receiving assistance. Her oldest brother was long since out of the house and sent money home when he could, but they had to hide even that small amount of income.

Jeanette and Archie's brother, Joe, were in the same grade during her school years. So Jeanette and Archie met through friends at school. "We didn't have dealings with each other, we just knew each other. Everybody in Shannon knew everybody. I had no inkling this would happen back then."

Jeanette majored in accounting in college at Alcorn, although she never practiced officially. "I chose Alcorn because my two brothers went down there. Plus, my home economics teacher from high school went to Alcorn and I loved her. She inspired me. I wanted to be like her."

Jeanette came to Milwaukee where her sister lived, to settle in and look for employment. "I stayed with my sister who still lives here, until I got married." Jeanette worked for thirty years at Blue Cross Blue Shield, and then in 2008, she was let go when the company downsized. She had spent decades working her way up the corporate ladder and being dismissed unceremoniously was painful. But it gave her time to shift her focus toward the church. As First Lady at New Hope, Jeanette believes her primary role is to exemplify God and live according to His word.

"She's a very straightforward person," explains Archie of his wife. "She doesn't argue, yet she always tells it like it is. Then she just goes about her business. When she's working on something, like flowers for the church or alterations or anything else, she gives it all her concentration."

For the first years of their marriage, the young family traveled only to visit their parents back in Shannon. That's how they spent their vacations. Not until all their parents had died did the couple finally take a honeymoon. They went to Minneapolis and left their two children under Jeanette's sister Mattie's care.

"We showed up in the city without any plans. Just found a hotel as we were approaching St. Paul and stayed there for two days. That was our belated honeymoon," laughs Archie.

The couple has since traveled extensively, to several states, and internationally. They've been to Turkey and Greece, then to Israel visiting the Holy Land, where they were baptized in the Jordan River. They've spent time in Orlando, Florida, with and without their grandkids. Myrtle Beach, South Carolina, is one of Jeanette's favorite trips because she loves to get up early in the morning and watch the sun rise over the ocean, the golden hour, and then take a walk on the beach.

Jeanette says Archie loves the word of God and loves people, even when they don't love him back. He always shows love, she says, no matter what.

"He's a God-fearing man and if he can help in any way, he will. He's a good-hearted person. He even loves his enemies."

As for their fifty-year marriage, she credits their success to give-and-take, open communication, and putting God first.

"If God gives you a mate, appreciate it and make the best of it."

Archie says readily, with a wide smile, that one of the happiest days of his life was April 15, 1971, the day his firstborn son, Reginald Demond Ivy, came into the world. By this time, Archie and Jeanette had been married two years. Reggie weighed eight pounds and ten ounces and was named by his mother. "A reddish looking fellow," Archie laughed.

One of Archie's last memories of his father was one of his first memories of his son. In August of 1971, when baby Reggie was just four months old, the small family drove down to Shannon to visit their parents. During this visit, Mose held his only grandchild. Unfortunately, it was the first and last time.

"To see my father hold that boy, to see the look on his face, the gleam in his eye was unforgettable. It was in this moment that we started to bond," whispers Archie. It was a painful short-lived reunion because Archie's father passed away on December 8, 1971.

When Reggie was almost three, the family's second child, Jeannece Marie, was born on March 18, 1974. Jeannece was seven pounds and eight ounces, a cute bundle of joy, also healthy. They now had two healthy children, a boy and a girl. Jeannece followed her brother everywhere, ignored the dolls people gave her as gifts, and went after Reggie's toys instead. When Jeannece was just one year old, Archie took his sabbatical and started commuting to get his Masters, and so began one of the most challenging periods of the family's history.

"At this point, we had two children bursting with energy and we thought we were done," said Archie.

But God had other plans. In 1976, Jeanette announced one day that she felt nauseous.

Andrea Patrice was born on February 11, 1977, weighing just over seven pounds, the smallest of the three kids. She was very active in the womb and continues to be very energetic to this day, according to her parents. "She has always been independent, with an I-can-do-it-myself attitude," says Archie

The couple tutored their kids at home using cards to teach the alphabet and numbers, the way Archie's mother had done for him, while making reading a regular part of every day. All three children did well in school and stayed out of trouble, though learning came easiest to Jeannece, Archie recalls.

Reggie was a healthy kid who laughed and threw fits of frustration in equal measure. Archie admits that Reggie was spoiled by his parents as well as by Archie's colleagues at school when Reggie used to tag along with his father during the work day. During preschool, Reggie fell in love with wrestling, and one day, when Archie picked him up, a teacher told him that Reggie had put another child in a choke hold.

"We gave him a serious talking-to that day," Archie recalled, even though he knew Reggie didn't intend to hurt the child.

"Reggie was a sensitive kid, always worried about others. He used to take pennies from the house to school with him," said Archie. "When we asked him why, he said he wanted to give them to the poor."

He had his mischievous side as well. When Reggie was about eight or nine, he made a big fuss about not going to church one Sunday. This was during a phase when Archie wasn't attending church regularly, and when Jeanette asked her son why he wouldn't go, Reggie strongly declared, "I'm not going to that stinking church. Daddy's not going so I'm not going."

That lit a fire under Archie, Jeanette disclosed, and he's gone to church ever since.

During middle school, Reggie was disciplined after skipping school with a friend. The school's assistant principal let Archie know directly after Reggie got caught playing hooky. Since Archie worked in the school system, Reggie probably should have known that he couldn't get away with it.

Another reckoning came one morning at the breakfast table, when Reggie used the G-D word after spending time with his uncle, Lenzo, who tended to use profane language rather freely.

Back in grade school, one of Reggie's white teachers told Archie and Jeanette he thought Reggie had a learning disability. He wanted Reggie to sit beside a white boy and learn from him, but Archie had a problem with that and refused to let it happen. And in high school, another white teacher told Archie that Reggie was having trouble learning, so Archie had his son transferred into the class of a Black teacher named Kenny Williams, a man Reggie had known most of his life. In Williams' class, things improved right away and Reggie quickly got back up to speed.

Reggie played basketball and football his freshman year, but Archie held firm that if any of his kids couldn't maintain a 2.5 GPA, they couldn't participate in sports. To make sure he maintained that GPA, Reggie cut back to just track for the rest of his high school career. He graduated from high school and immediately enrolled in Carroll University in Waukesha, Wisconsin, where he majored in communications and marketing. He continued to run track throughout college and Archie traveled all over to watch him compete.

After college, Reggie worked briefly for a national car rental firm. Archie said he quit when he realized that he couldn't meet his quotas unless he sold insurance to people who didn't need it. This wasn't how he wanted to live. So, he started working as an educational assistant in the Milwaukee Public School system, then went back for his Masters in Curriculum and Instruction.

"He's become an excellent teacher," beams Archie with pride.

Starting in college, Reggie became active in the choir and then became a choir director at New Hope Church.

"He's one of the best directors you'll find," Archie added.

Reggie and his wife Debbie have been happily married since 2002. They have two kids, Archie's only grandchildren. Taylor Jenae was born October 24, 2005. "She's fourteen but thinks she's 20," said Archie. And Caleb Reginald was born in 2007. They attend Milwaukee School of Languages, the school where their father teaches math and science. Their mom is a preschool and first grade teacher at Burbank Elementary.

When Reggie talks about his father, he hardly knows where to start, because he says there are so many stories to tell. The first thing he recalls about his father during his childhood is that he was a stern disciplinarian, but on the other hand also a very loving father.

"I remember coming home with a bad report card," says Reggie, "and he was really upset about it because I'd dropped several grades in one class. He came at me with a belt, and I can laugh about it now because when he tried to whoop me, I caught the belt in mid-air. I felt like a Kung Fu master, but he wasn't too impressed."

Afterwards, Archie told him that the really disappointing thing was that he had the ability to easily earn a good grade. He knew he could achieve, so there was really no excuse.

"Dad was always a straight shooter," adds Reggie. Now that he's saying many of the same things he heard as a child to his own children, like "Be your best and do your best," for example, he understands his own father better.

Reggie's grades improved, though he was never an Honor Roll kid. All Archie wanted was for him to put forth the effort, even if he fell short.

If he could change anything about his childhood, Reggie reflects, he would have had his father around more. "He wasn't like an absentee father or anything," explains Reggie, "but he was a hard worker, and he was always out providing for us. There were times when I needed him and he wasn't there, because he was working."

Of the many memories Reggie has of his father, the ones he cherishes the most are in recent memory.

"Every time we get an opportunity to hang out, we play golf together. I appreciate those times, and then as silly as it may sound, sometimes when I'm over there, and we're just watching a ballgame together, times where it's truly only father and son, not two ministers just sitting there talking. I appreciate his wisdom that he gives me as a minister but when we are just father and son, I love it."

At the moment, Archie has the better golf game, admitted Reggie. "He has the advantage of being able to play more than I do. But I'm catching up."

As for memories he'd prefer to forget, Reggie recalls the time in his father's career when he was dismissed from Christian Union Church. "It was disturbing for me because that was my first time seeing people turn on him."

Reggie hasn't seen his father show much vulnerability in his lifetime, not even after a major disappointment.

"In front of us and his family, he has to show that tough exterior. But inside, I know things bother him. There's so much sacrifice required of him, and people just don't quite understand sometimes the things that he has to go through."

Reggie, who has been around for all of his father's tenure at New Hope, cites the recent renovation at the church as his father's greatest accomplishment.

"That was something that at first, people did not see could happen, so when it came about, it kind of opened people's eyes, that hey, this man can take this church to another level. From there it has opened a lot of doors and a lot of eyes."

Reggie is used to being the son of a pastor, even a well-known one, by this point. But it's still a surprise when he tells someone his name and they recognize it.

"'Man, let me tell you about your dad,' people will say. And then they'll tell me stories. In his own way, Dad has put his imprint on the city of Milwaukee. Because every time they mention my dad's name, it's always something positive, it's always something good about how he helped them out, or how he helped the community out."

As for stories Archie might not tell on himself, Reggie has no trouble sharing that his father is one of the most playfully sarcastic people he's ever met. "He does it to me, he does it to my sister, and he even does it to his own wife. If you open the door, he's going to go through it. If I call the house and he answers the phone and I say, 'Oh, you're home,' he'll say, 'No, I'm not, this is your mama with a deep voice.'"

These days, Reggie is mostly concerned that his father takes care of himself. "There was a point where he was constantly giving and giving and giving, and I was worried he would burn out. He gave so much to the church; it was his second home. But now I see him spending more time with my mom, there's time for them to take vacations, and he's really making sure he's spending more quality time with the family. I appreciate him doing that."

At this stage of Archie's career, Reggie's primary worry is that his father might not be ready to hand over the reins and trust others with the church community he's spent so much of his time and energy growing.

"I'm not saying that he doesn't trust people, and I'm not saying he micro-manages, but he still wants to be in-the-know, and then he always gives a suggestion instead of backing off and trusting people to handle the tasks he's assigned."

Reggie is now a father himself and still describes his father as his greatest role model, including how to love and respect women.

"I've seen my mom and dad have disagreements, but I have never ever in my lifetime seen my dad disrespect her. Never. He got in trouble one time for forgetting to pick her up, but he never disrespected her. Always loved her. And always, he knew when to kind of step back when my mom put her foot down. He knew went to assert and when to regress."

Archie is a devoted grandfather to Reggie's kids, who call him Pawpaw.

"They love him, and he loves them. He claims he doesn't spoil them, but you know he's a grandfather, so he uses that tactfully, but on the other hand, he's quick to discipline, like he was with us. They know what Pawpaw expects."

It wasn't easy being a preacher's kid, facing the pressure and expectations from everyone in the community. "Some of my friends gave me a hard time about it. In high school, that's where I really felt it, because that's when people kind of really realized that my dad was a minister. Or you know, if I let a curse word slip out, they would say they'd tell my dad, and it kind of wore on me. When I have other friends who are preacher's kids, I see them kind of rebelling, I can understand."

When Reggie reflects on his father's life, he considers Archie's journey. "If you just try to envision yourself going through his journey, you come to realize that with God, all things are possible. Put your mind to your goals, and you can achieve them. And I want people to really understand that, when they read his story. I want people to keep that in the forefront of their minds as they walk with him through this journey."

According to Archie, Jeannece was the most introverted of his children. She was quiet, direct, and sometimes gave the impression of being stern, though she's not. Although she was a friendly child, according to Jeanette, she wore a look on her face like she was unhappy. "We love you!" Jeanette would say to Jeannece to cheer her up.

"She was always a perfectionist," explains Archie. "Never much of a social butterfly. She participated in basketball as a freshman and sophomore, and track and field throughout high school and was pretty good."

Jeannece graduated with honors and attended Jackson State like her father, though he didn't pressure her to follow in his footsteps. She pledged the Delta sorority while at Jackson State. During college, Archie would send her bus tickets to visit both of her grandmothers in Shannon during spring break.

She graduated Magna Cum Laude in math and computer science, and then became a math teacher in the Milwaukee Public Schools. Archie helped her by introducing her to a colleague whose school needed good math teachers. Jeannece took to the work and settled in. Although she'd planned to return for her Masters in math, she has continued to teach while working on advanced teaching certification. She has served as track coach at Marshall High School, Hamilton High School, and is presently the Head Track Coach at Madison High School. She spends summers volunteering as an AAU track coach with the Running Rebels.

Andrea, the most outgoing of the three Ivy children, is the one who never stops surprising Archie. "She's never met a stranger," he said. "Our social butterfly," recalls Jeanette. "Andrea was rebellious and always knew her own mind, and has always been her own person."

The sisters are like night and day, according to their parents. As a child, Andrea played all the time with her dolls. She'd line them up and pretend to be their teacher, and chastised them when they acted up. She tried to follow her siblings across the street and into the neighborhood even as a baby in diapers. Like her siblings, she ran track in high school, and was also a cheerleader.

"She got more whippings than the other two put together," reveals Archie about Andrea. In high school, Archie took away her license because she broke curfew.

Andrea was active in track and field, and theater during middle and high school, and her passion for it grew during her years at the University of Minnesota, where she majored in public health. She worked in the public health field after graduating, but acting is still her first love, and over the years she's appeared in promotions, commercials, and many plays. Archie is not sure where Andrea got her love for acting, but he'd like to think that both he and Jeanette had a little influence since they both participated in school plays in high school.

She has an agent and is a member of the Actors Guild, which is no small feat. Several years ago, Archie and Jeanette drove her out to Los Angeles so she could pursue her acting career. She returned to Milwaukee after two years, but keeps a flexible work schedule as an office worker with the Milwaukee school system so she can travel to Chicago, Los Angeles, and New York to accept acting jobs as they come up.

"Of the three, Andrea has pushed me the most to write a book about my life," said Archie. "She's always felt that my story might inspire others."

Archie and Jeanette agreed to help their kids for two years after college. They provided each one a car and a place to live in a townhouse on 85th Street in Milwaukee. Reggie lived on one side and Jeannece on the other until Reggie married. Now that Andrea is back in Milwaukee, she lives on the second side.

Andrea has quite a few stories she could share about her father. But the one that comes to mind first is about a time when they were all down in Mississippi for a family reunion, driving in the car, and her father and uncle noticed a huge turtle crossing the street.

"They stop and get out of the car, and they put the turtle in the back of my uncle's car and we drive to my uncle's house with the turtle in the back. I'm thinking, since my uncle has like, cows and horses, you know, and pigs, that he's just adding a turtle! So, it's Saturday, that's the day they did that, and Sunday morning, we wake up to go to church and there's turtle for breakfast."

This was a typical story, says Andrea. "It was just like him. When he loves something, he loves it. He and my uncle had a serious taste for turtle, and that's what they did. I think it took him back to his childhood, because he hadn't eaten turtle for a long while."

Another time, Andrea stepped on a line of fire ants down in Mississippi, and she got so scared she wouldn't let go of her father's leg. He couldn't shake her off. "He was my protector, always," she says.

There were times, though, that Andrea recalls that his dedication to his work was confusing to her as a child, when she wanted him home and he couldn't be.

"As you get older, you understand, but as a child you don't."

At her high school graduation, Archie could only attend part of the ceremony.

"He never saw me walk across the stage because he was Principal at North Division and he had to get to the school."

Once, Andrea and her father watched *The Lion King* together, and the memory stayed in her mind because it was the first time she'd cried watching a movie.

"It was the moment Mufasa died, and it was very interesting to me because Mufasa stood for the same thing that my father stood for, to me. Not that my dad's the king of the jungle by any means, but to me he was, he symbolized that. I realized that he meant so much to so many, just like Mufasa meant so much to so many in the jungle. So, it's like he had all these obligations, including teaching Simba to be a responsible leader. And like with my father, he taught not just my siblings but me as well, not just by what he said but by what he did."

As the most outgoing and adventurous of the three children, Andrea sometimes bore the brunt of her father's strict discipline. In those times, she felt their personalities had a tendency to clash.

"Sometimes he doesn't understand. For example, I'm an actor. He doesn't get what that means sometimes. He's more about, 'Ok, so, you go to college, you get a job, you do this.' Because he's a firm believer in education."

Andrea is very aware that her father treats his work and his pastorate with the same firm hand as his children.

"His philosophy is, if you disagree with me, you can go read for yourself. He's a firm believer in you developing your own relationship with God and wanting you to find your path in your walk with God, and he's there to guide you and help you. I lived in Minnesota for years and also in L.A. I always have to stop comparing people's different styles of preaching to my father's, because I'm used to a teacher style. I'm not used to somebody yelling at me all day and not really saying much. Where's the meat? What am I getting out of it? And I really think that harkens to his emphasis on education and trying to help people grow as a Christian and in this walk with God.

My mom keeps telling me, 'you're not gonna find anybody like your dad.' They've been together for 50 years and it's just a beautiful thing!"

Most people see her father as a mentor, a teacher, a pastor, a reverend, but for Andrea, he's a father first and foremost.

"People can always get another pastor or appoint another pastor, but at the end of the day, that's my father and I support everything he does. I know that the footprint he leaves and the shadow he casts across this community is a great one."

Growing up, Andrea felt the extra pressure of being the preacher's kid. When she went to church, it was a spectacle, she says, and she felt people were looking at her like she was under a microscope.

"They could have a niece or a sibling that's a dancer at a strip club, but let me once go have a glass of wine with a friend and they're like, 'Oh my God! Did you see Pastor Ivy's daughter with that drink in her hand?'"

Archie knew from the start that he wasn't going to raise his kids the way he'd been raised, without hugs and affection from his father. He was a demonstrative father in the early years, always picking up the kids and hugging them. But he was distracted, too, by his career and his struggle with his calling to ministry. One of his few regrets is that he was away from home too much during these years and the burden of raising the children fell on Jeanette's shoulders.

Jeanette is not only the love of Archie's life and his best friend, but she's also the First Lady of their church. Recently, at a lunch in Green Lake, a woman asked Archie where the First Lady was that day, and he told her Jeanette had work back at the church.

"But First Ladies don't do anything but look pretty!" joked the woman.

Archie said to her, "That's not my wife. She rolls up her sleeves."

To Jeanette, the title of First Lady doesn't mean anything, or at least doesn't mean she's not an equal member of the church, carrying her own weight. She works in the kitchen, vacuums the floors, and pitches in wherever help is needed. She's a member of the choir and teaches Sunday school, too.

Because of their strong religious beliefs, Archie and Jeanette believe that marriage is a sacrament and therefore they do not believe in divorce. They try never to go to sleep with anger in their hearts.

"Neither of us could get any good sleep that way, anyway," said Archie.

These days, when she's not involved in one of her church's many activities, Jeanette likes to go to the movies, read, sew, and is not afraid of getting her hands dirty working around the house. Archie told the story of how she took the front door off its hinges, removed the old paint, and repainted it.

"She wouldn't let me just buy a new door, because she prides herself on being pretty handy," chuckled Archie. "And it really looks nice."

Fifty years later, Archie has nothing but good things to say about his choice of life partner. "We have a wonderful marriage. One reason is because of the work we both continue to do, year after year, to mature together and adjust to each other."

"The church readily gave her the title of First Lady," added Archie. "It's a secular title, not a biblical one. This means that although Jeanette has no special privileges in the church, she's heavily involved and has earned the respect of our congregants. She's very dedicated, very involved. She's faithful and appreciated. She's serious about the Bible and preparing her lessons and being a godly wife. I often bounce ideas off her because she's my harshest critic."

Jeanette and Archie have worked to be on the same page in terms of how to raise their kids. Given Jeanette's fatherless childhood, it was particularly important that they were both engaged, loving parents. Archie worked too much, he knows, but they always took the kids with them when they traveled and rarely left them with others. The family didn't take fancy vacations when the kids were little, because the family struggled in those days, but they did what they could. And they always took them back to Shannon to see their grandparents during spring and summer break. "It was important to me that my kids understood their roots," says Archie.

After settling into his career as a pastor, Archie turned his attention back to his children, perhaps to a degree that keeps them too dependent on him in some ways. "I think the reason my daughters aren't married is because they're looking for me in a man, and they're not going to find it," he says.

"They have me on a pedestal. I wish for Jeannece that she could become more assertive and self-sufficient, because she's very insightful and has a great mind. And I wish that Andrea would check in more often, because she's so busy and sometimes we lose track of her."

That said, Archie has a solid relationship with all of his children.

Archie believes that as close as the family is today, his children would describe him as fair, loving, affectionate, a good role model, but also over-protective. They would say that he didn't spend enough time with them when they were children, though he's been trying to make up for that since.

"I wish my kids had more of me growing up. I was so busy working as a football official in the fall, basketball official during the winter, and baseball in the spring and summer, plus working part time at Pabst brewery during the summer. I wish I hadn't been so transient. That's a regret I have, and I've apologized to them for it," Archie revealed.

He has struggled, too, with the choice both of his daughters have made to remain unmarried, a choice they both say suits them just fine for now.

"Sometimes I wonder if I did something wrong," he reflects. "Maybe because I was a good father and husband that they are looking for another me and overlooking a good mate. But it's their choice, I know. I am sorry there won't be more grandchildren. I worry that they won't have children to take care of them as they age. But they are comfortable where they are in life, which is the most important thing."

Young Pastor Ivy at Providence Missionary Baptist Church

On the left Pastor Ivy's Cousin Hosea Foster and Pastor Archie Ivy

Archie with a Student at Milwaukee Technical School

Jeannece, Archie, Andrea, Reginald and Jeanette Ivy

Jimmie Trimble, Archie's lifelong friend   Archie and his cousin Jack Edmond

Archie's dad, Mose, his mother Ruby and his sister Darlene

Archie's younger twin brothers: Jack and Jesse Ivy

Archie and his mother Ruby Ivy

Mama Ollie

Archie and high school referee friends

Wedding picture with Jeanette Ivy, Archie Ivy and Archie's
first cousins: Arvella Gardner and Lowella Hatton

Wedding photo of Archie and Jeanette Ivy

Jeannece Ivy (oldest daughter), Pastor Archie Ivy, First Lady-
Jeanette Ivy, and Andrea Ivy (youngest daughter).

50ᵗʰ Wedding Anniversary: Jeanette Ivy and Archie Ivy

New Hope Missionary Baptist Church Members with the Ivy
family celebrating their 50ᵗʰ wedding anniversary

Ivy Family 50ᵗʰ Wedding Anniversary

Farm life in Shannon, MS

Family gathering at Archie's mother's (Ruby Ivy) house on Easter

Archie's Aunt Larabelle and GrandMama Ollie

Family Trip to Myrtle Beach, SC

Archie delivering an uplifting sermon at New Hope

Pastor Ivy and Pastor Crouthers
earn their doctorate degrees

Pastor Ivy and wife Jeanette
with grandkids Taylor and
Caleb Ivy at Church

Archie with son Reginald, grandson Caleb and brother Mose

Rev. Carmen Porco, Rev. Archie Ivy and Rev. Roy Nabors

Archie with grandkids in 2008: Taylor on the left and Caleb on the right

Church Services at New Hope Missionary Baptist Church

Pastor Ivy in robe he wears to perform weddings

Pastor Ivy sharing both the cultural and spiritual aspects of the Black Church

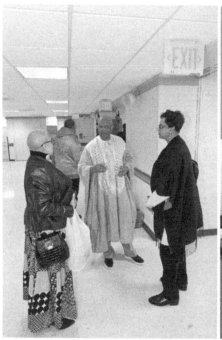

Pastor Ivy discussing church
activities with members

Pastor Ivy teaching at church

Lunch with friends: Pastors Archie Ivy, Fred Crouthers and Pastor Williamson

CHAPTER NINE
Bargain With God

"For God so loved the world, that he gave his only begotten Son, that whosoever believeth in him should not perish, but have everlasting life" –John 3:16

Archie had made a life for himself in Milwaukee, and by the time he left teaching to become a principal, his family was growing and they were putting down roots. That said, the 1970s were a turbulent time for Archie's emotional life, in terms of his own spirituality. He wrestled with the calling that he felt he had received from God. He never forgot his once-in-a-lifetime, all-encompassing feeling of bliss and love that enveloped him on his grandmother's porch when he was just nine years old. It was both powerful and peaceful. It emboldened him to step uniquely forward, for his age, and give his life to Christ. Since then, he'd even tried to disqualify himself in God's eyes by steering from his Bible lessons and drinking and partying. But he knew deep down that all he was doing was postponing the inevitable.

"There was something missing in my life, and I was bothered by it," Archie explained about the 1970s. "I was restless. I was trying to fit where I didn't quite fit. With my son Reggie's birth and my father's death, both in 1971, I knew I needed to make a change, but I still put it off."

In 1972, Archie's spiritual unrest grew too powerful to ignore. During the summers, when school was out, Archie worked third shift on the line at Pabst Brewing. One summer night, he was watching the beer bottles coming down the line, and all of a sudden, he started sobbing uncontrollably and couldn't stop.

"It came to me just like we're talking here," recalled Archie. "It was time for me to make a decision about my calling."

He tried to make a deal with God. He told God if he could earn his PhD by the age of 33, he'd follow his calling. But he hadn't even earned his Master's degree yet, so he wondered if this was just another way of stalling. If he was to keep his bargain with God, Archie knew he would have to take some concrete steps toward his education.

He decided to talk to colleagues in the Milwaukee Public Schools about the idea of taking a sabbatical. This would give him the time he needed to earn a Master's degree. He was told that it would take at least a year for his application to be approved. Archie applied in November of 1974, hoping to hold on long enough to keep his promises to himself and to God.

Surprisingly, Archie's application was approved almost immediately. He talked to friends and colleagues about his Masters options, and in the end, he settled on the University of Wisconsin in Platteville, which was relatively close, a two-and-a-half-hour drive from Milwaukee. UW-Platteville was also the alma mater of Marshall Bullock, an assistant principal at Robert Fulton, whom Archie admired.

At this stage in his life, Archie had a wife and two children, and had just bought a little Opal station wagon. Leaving his job for graduate school meant cutting his salary in half. It was a hard time for the whole family, especially Jeanette, since he was living in Platteville during the week and coming home only on the weekends.

"People told Jeanette that they didn't think she should let me go, but she knew it was something I needed to do," Archie declared. "When we got married, we knew we were bound to each other forever, a lifetime commitment. She made a big sacrifice when I went away to graduate school, and in spite of the negativity from friends, she never showed any concern. She just went to work and took care of the kids and rarely complained."

People also told him it wasn't realistic and probably couldn't even be done, to finish all thirty credits for his Masters in just one year. But Archie was determined and he pushed himself so hard that when he came home for semester break, he almost had a nervous breakdown. He sat down at the kitchen table with his textbooks and started shaking uncontrollably. He'd started to experience this heightened anxiety at school, but at home it became overwhelming. He called his family doctor, who told him to come immediately to the clinic.

"It was the pressure," Archie recalls. "My nerves and the stress—I'd made myself sick."

The doctor forced Archie to face the fact that if he continued at this pace, he would most likely end up having a nervous breakdown. Archie wouldn't agree to change his self-imposed deadline because he needed to finish school as soon as he could and return supporting his family financially. However, he did agree to take two weeks off. Remarkably, the extended family time and rest were just what he needed. Afterwards, he felt back to normal.

During this demanding time at UW-Platteville, Archie leaned heavily on his faith and asked God to give him the strength to make it through. In the end, he met his goal of finishing all thirty credits in one year.

"I was the only person of color in my graduating class," said Archie. "God gave me the strength I needed not only to endure but to succeed."

After his graduation, Archie had a new degree and a new job. He returned to full-time teaching at Milwaukee Trade and Technical High

School under the leadership of Dr. Hal Zerbal, who hired him to teach mechanical drafting.

Archie had more than eight years under his teaching belt at this point, but the school had its own pecking order. Archie was assigned classes in three different classrooms, as far apart from each other as they could be. His second year there, the teachers went on strike. Archie, who felt strongly that his job was to teach, not to mention that he still hadn't recovered financially from the sabbatical and needed the money, crossed the picket line.

"The other teachers were furious," Archie disclosed. "They even picketed my house. But the thing they were picketing for wasn't about me. My job was to teach children."

It took several years to end the animosity and build back the trust with the other teachers, who continued to rebuke Archie with small gestures, like parking in his parking space and trying to lock him in the men's restroom.

"Those years were frustrating for me. I knew who was trying to anger me and I told them not to mess with me. I never bothered anyone. I didn't hang out in the lunchroom, I just kept to myself and ate lunch in my class-room. The other teachers who had crossed the picket line still talked to me, but that was it for a while. I lost a lot of ground in the pecking order, even though I'd been teaching for years."

Today, he realizes that he might have been missing the larger picture of what the teachers' strike was all about: better working conditions and pay for all teachers, which is now the kind of thing he believes could be just what the school system needs. He respects protests, generally speaking, but he believed he was doing what was right for his students at the time. "You have to let people know who you are and what you stand for," Archie said defiantly.

During his years teaching at Milwaukee Trade and Tech, Archie was troubled by the deal he'd made with God. He knew deep down that he was still running from the calling he'd received when he was nine years old, and this internal struggle was starting to affect him physically.

"Some days, I felt so sick that just lying on the floor looked good to me," he flatly stated. "I was making myself sick by running from the Lord, running from my calling."

He went to the doctor, who could find nothing wrong with him.

Jeanette saw her husband wrestling with his calling. She was the primary witness to Archie's winding path toward the ministry over the years. He would turn to her when he was ready, she believed. She noticed his agitation, how he kept himself very busy, was never home, and was quick to lose his temper. Yet, she never forced him to make a decision and she always tried to be supportive. She had faith that he would find his way.

One night, he was spending a rare evening at home when his daughter mindlessly stepped over him to ask her mother for some help with her homework. "Why not ask your father?" said Jeanette, and their daughter looked genuinely surprised and answered, "Why, is he here?"

It was a moment Archie will never forget. "I was keeping myself so busy, trying to fill that void that I had neglected my own children."

Around this time, Archie and Jeanette found themselves a spiritual home at the Providence Baptist Church, which was quite a distance from their new home located on 90th Street. They visited three times before joining.

By 1978, the ill feelings from the teacher strike were behind him. Archie was back at work, bowling with other teachers on Wednesdays after work, popular with his students, and active in the church and community.

He had some friends who'd completed a PhD program in Urban Leadership, which interested him. He requested an application and filled it out. His dream of earning a doctorate was still very much alive but then, as he puts it, God put on the brakes.

"He had something else in store for me," Archie said about God's intervention.

Archie didn't pursue the Urban Leadership program but he said he was in spiritual turmoil for three more years until 1981. By this time, he was a Deacon at Providence Baptist and was in charge of the Christian education program, a position he earned by combining his teaching experience with his expert knowledge of the Bible.

In 1981, Archie attended the National Baptist Congress of Christian Education in Omaha, Nebraska. It was a weeklong program of classes and seminars, and in one small group, a man whom Archie had only just met turned to him and asked why he hadn't gone on to do what he was called to do—be a minister.

"He said he saw it in me. Still today, people can see it in me. 'You're a pastor,' they say. Even back then, people saw something in me that I couldn't see in myself."

He had believed, from talking to others that the calling only comes in the form of white lights and dramatic appearances. His calling was just as real, but it came as a quiet force.

"I was never out of my body. Mine was more of an internal experience, an unexpected overwhelming yet calming bliss and love that I knew came from God. It was a feeling inside I had to investigate but nothing wild and dramatic like some preachers claim."

Archie believed it was God's will, but he still wasn't yet ready. He wanted to be better, not because he judged others but because he judged himself. He'd seen men at the Baptist convention slip out to drink whiskey in the back of the building. He'd been known to have a drink of scotch, or Crown Royal every now and then, and a few beers while mowing the grass. He prayed for grace to overcome his shortcomings. Eventually, as part of his transition toward accepting the calling, he poured two cases of Pabst beer down the drain and gave up smoking, which he'd done regularly since he was a senior in high school.

"I asked God to take smoking away from me in 1967, and He did. Now, I was asking God to take the taste of alcohol out of my mouth. That was a big step toward me accepting my calling," he recalled.

Archie left Omaha feeling excited by his learning but also guilty and conflicted. The feeling wasn't new to him, but it was growing intolerable. Back in Milwaukee, he continued to work in his roles at the church, and after a few months, a younger congregant announced his formal call to the ministry during the service. Archie was chagrined; the young man had managed to do the one thing Archie hadn't yet done.

The next day, Archie called Rev. Joe A. Games, the pastor of Providence Baptist Church and asked for a meeting. When he walked through the door, the pastor said, "I've been waiting for you."

"I'm ready to accept my call to ministry," said Archie, giving voice to what had always been his destiny. When it finally happened, Jeanette felt immensely relieved. Finally, they both could move forward and relax.

"She had been one-hundred-percent supportive, and it paid off," said Archie gratefully.

Archie's calling and his response had a profound effect on his life. He'd always felt that he was different from other people, and others had always seen something in him that set him apart.

He had believed for years that his calling was to teach, to help kids. Even when he started to accept his call to the ministry, he didn't think he'd become a pastor. He believed he was best suited to be a Christian educator. "That's a calling, too, and I was already doing it," said Archie.

But there was no avoiding the fact that he was called to do both: teach and pastor. "Maybe I'm unique. Not every pastor is a teacher and not every teacher is a pastor. But I'm both, and that was a gift to me from God."

For others who receive the call, however subtly, he has some advice:

"Don't waste your time bargaining with God. Yield to him and do what He wants. I don't feel I wasted that decade, but I do wonder where I would be if I'd made the decision earlier. God eased me where he wanted me to be, and he prepared me for it. He always has a plan, a process, and a purpose. He had a plan for me even before I was born. I'm here by assignment!"

CHAPTER TEN
Becoming A Pastor

"Thy word is a lamp unto my feet, and a light
unto my path."–Psalm 119:105

After finally ending his years of indecision and restlessness, Archie's first attempt to find a pastorate in 1986 wasn't the hearty welcome into the ministry that he imagined. He applied for a pastorship in Chicago and was one of two finalists. The St. Paul Missionary Baptist Church vote resulted in a split decision on the part of the hiring committee. Archie took his name out of the hat even though he was asked to apply again. He didn't want to start his ministry with a split church community, knowing that half of the church wanted someone else to lead them.

"I didn't want to come into a situation where the congregation was divided," he said, giving voice to the reasonable way of thinking that's always been his signature.

It proved to be the right decision on Archie's part. In November of 1988, Pastor Paul McHenry of Christian Union Baptist Church in Milwaukee asked Archie to breakfast to talk about a possible pastoral position at his church. He was ill and wanted Archie to succeed him. Pastor McHenry asked Archie to lead a workshop and then preach a sermon so the Christian Union congregation would get to know him better. Obviously, Archie made a good impression because in July of 1989, he became the new pastor of Christian Union Baptist Church.

It was his first time leading a church, and the position came with complications. First of all, Pastor McHenry was still living and the pastorate had been his only source of income. Archie made a deal with the church leaders: they would keep McHenry in his church-owned home and continue to pay his salary until he passed, at which point McHenry's entire salary would transfer to Archie. According to Archie, this was a handshake deal, and he had no reason to think it wouldn't be honored when the time came.

At Christian Union, Archie found that the skills he'd been sharpening in all his years as a teacher and administrator—people skills, writing and speaking skills, leadership skills—transferred smoothly to his new role as pastor. However, Archie says Christian Union was a church set in its ways, informally led by a matriarch and her family. It was evident from the start that he wouldn't be able to call many shots, at least not without a lot of opposition and second-guessing.

For example, when he moved into his church office, Archie needed a bookshelf so he bought himself one out of the church's budget. He was immediately told that he had no right to make that kind of purchase decision. Archie was baffled and disheartened. Every time he came to the leaders with an idea or vision, he found out later that they held meetings afterward behind his back, to discuss what they thought of his ideas without his input.

Despite the micro-managing, Archie held to his faith that he was in the right place. Over time, he was able to inspire his congregants, impose structure, develop staff personnel, and acquire property for the church. These were modest improvements albeit remarkable, considering he was working with so much opposition and red tape.

When he looks back at the time in his first pastorate at Christian Union, Archie can see clearly a series of signs telling him that Christian Union was not his final stop. Markedly, it was the way Jeanette was treated by church members. "She never felt comfortable there, as the pastor's wife, and she was never recognized or consulted by church members," Archie explained.

There were other reasons why Christian Union did not turn out to be the pastorate home Archie was seeking. There was significant opposition to his broad vision for the church's future, for one thing. The betrayal over Pastor McHenry's salary was another reason, Archie claims. The Church's Executive Board failed to keep its promise to Archie when Pastor McHenry died. They were supposed to increase Archie's salary by the amount they had paid McHenry but refused to do so. If Archie hadn't been teaching at the time which brought in additional income, he probably would have left Christian Union earlier than he did.

One night, he had a dream in which weeds were growing up around the church members. This was a premonition, he believes. He was trying to pull the church forward, but the congregation had grown stagnant. He had taken Christian Union as far as he could. He had been approached by a member of The New Hope Missionary Baptist Church in January 1995 about an opening. The current pastor was retiring. He'd been invited to the New Hope church to give a sermon in February, then invited back on Palm Sunday to teach a class. By June, they'd have an offer for him, church leaders told him—but June came and went.

That summer, Archie attended a Baptist conference in San Diego and realized that word had gotten out that he was a candidate for the pastor opening at New Hope. This bit of gossip had unfortunately made it back to his congregation at Christian Union. Then in August, Archie bumped into a deacon from New Hope. He immediately referred to Archie as *Pastor Ivy*, a signal of respect that instilled Archie with the confidence to ask the deacon what was taking them so long to offer him the job. They were working on it, Archie was told.

Once word made its way to the matriarch of Christian Union's most powerful family, that he was being seriously considered for the position at New Hope, his church colleagues confronted Archie. He told them until he received an official offer from New Hope, he was still the pastor of Christian Union and that was that.

Finally, New Hope officially offered him the pastorate. Archie gave ninety days' notice to Christian Union, so there would be a smooth transition and plenty of time to interview potential candidates. But the church leaders weren't having it. They rejected his notice and instead gave him a week's worth of pay and terminated him that day. They told him to clean out his office. It was a rough ending to a position where he'd never felt entirely welcome or comfortable.

But Archie was ready for a new start. He began his ministry at New Hope the first Sunday of November, 1995.

"And here I still am, twenty-five years later," he laughed.

When Archie reminisces about pastors who helped him learn the ins and outs of becoming a pastor, he has strong praise for Rev. Paul McHenry, who handed over the reins at Christian Union.

"He knew I was going to succeed him. He showed me how to work with congregants, how to be humble and how to be generous."

McHenry didn't have the education that Archie had, but he had the experience Archie hadn't yet earned, so Archie listened to the man and took his lessons to heart. After Archie became the pastor of Christian Union, McHenry moved his membership from Mount Carmel to Christian Union, so Archie could be his pastor. This was a great vote of confidence, Archie felt, and he told the congregation that he was humbled. Typically Baptist ministers held personal church memberships outside their own church, since they couldn't minister to themselves. McHenry's move was especially poignant to Archie.

Another important mentor was Reverend Genoa Patterson, whom Archie met when he was part of a minister's union established by his friend, Dr. Fred Croutherss, well before Archie had his own pastorate. It was a fellowship and ministry consisting of non-pastors and associate ministers. The advisors to the group were Rev. Genoa Patterson and Rev. Bendel Nichols, both of whom would play significant roles in Archie's development as a pastor.

"They taught us what pastoralship was all about; how to work with people, and how to be a God-fearing pastor."

He also learned from Rev. Patterson to be careful not to unintentionally take advantage of members of the congregation, how to be honest and studious, how to work with other pastors, and how to cultivate mutual respect. Rev. Patterson often invited Archie to teach and preach at his church, to observe him and mentor Archie "from the pew."

Reverend Bendel Nichols offered Archie the wisdom of his experience, with advice on how to be faithful to his family and wife, how to set a good example in the community, and how not to yield to temptation even when you find yourself in vulnerable positions.

Reverend Leroy Mixon was another astute and highly educated mentor of Archie's who believed fervently in Christian education and taught Archie the nuts and bolts of church administration, lessons that would prove invaluable throughout his ministry. He taught Archie how a church can function like a well-run business, and how to put people into appropriate church positions according to their skills and interests.

"I learned all of my practical lessons from other pastors, not from seminary. By the time I got to seminary, I already knew a lot, sometimes more than the teachers, just from experience and listening to smart people," Archie offered.

And in his early years after seminary, Reverend Floyd Jones, was one of the first pastors who gave Archie the opportunity to preach in his church. Rev. Jones pastored Bethlehem Church in Milwaukee, and when he went on vacation, he left Archie the responsibility of his congregation, as did Reverend Lawrence Presley.

"When it comes to preaching, you need opportunities to exercise your gifts, and Rev. Jones gave me more opportunities than anyone else."

CHAPTER ELEVEN

The Theology That Guides Him

---

*"Come to me, all you who are weary and burdened,
and I will give you rest"* –Matthew 11:28

The song "Give Me That Old Time Religion" comes to mind when trying to describe Archie's religious beliefs and practices. He grew up in the Mississippi Black church with down home preaching, shouting, clapping, and giving praise to the Lord. Although he describes his preaching style more like a teacher than a traditional fiery Baptist preacher, at heart, he is still a fundamentalist.

He believes that the Bible is the true word of God. That Jesus was born from a virgin and that Christ's death was the atonement for our sins. Rev. Ivy believes that Jesus rose from the grave and that he will return some day in glory to take his followers back with him to heaven.

He believes that each of us will be judged for our sins and those who profess a belief in Jesus will be saved and those who don't will be condemned to eternal hell. As a Baptist, Archie believes that faith is a matter between God and the individual.

Baptism (full immersion) is one of his fundamental beliefs because it symbolizes the cleansing of our sins. The Baptist church believes in baptism only after a person has professed Christ as their Savior. The practice stems from the disciples' baptism in John 3 and in Romans 6, which say Christians are "buried with him through baptism into death in order that, just as Christ was raised from the dead through the glory of the Father, we too may live a new life."

New Hope Missionary Baptist Church, like most Baptist churches, hosts the Lord's Supper, also known as communion, monthly, to honor the death of Jesus. The practice comes from Jesus' Last Supper with his disciples. At communion, bread and "wine" are traditionally served. The bread symbolizes the purity and body of Christ and the wine (typically grape juice) symbolizes the blood of Christ that was shed for our sins.

Archie underscores that Baptists believe in missionary work and encourage each other to share their faith openly and take the message of Christ to their neighbors, workplaces, schools, and into their daily lives. Baptists also believe in salvation by grace through faith. This means to them, that all humans have sinned and are in need of salvation, but cannot do anything to save themselves. Instead, God saves people through his grace, so long as they have faith in him.

"We are spiritual, and we are of the flesh," Archie says about his spiritual journey. "Life deals us ups and downs, and we have burdens, but our burdens don't define us. My spiritual side helps me deal with my human side. That's the power of my connection to God.

In 2004, Archie and Jeanette visited Israel and the Holy Land on a ten-day study tour. He wanted to make the journey, he says, to authenticate all he'd read about the life of Christ. He also wanted to get a sense for what life might have been like for Christ and the apostles, to see Mount Galilee and Mount Olive, where Christ ministered.

"The places where Christ walked are real places. The places Paul walked are real places. Because I've been there, I have a vivid picture in mind that helps me see it the way it's always been. The spiritual struggle is nothing new in human existence; it's always been there. Visiting the places where He lived and died reminds me of that."

Archie believes the trip aided his spiritual growth and gave him a broader understanding of how Christianity fits into world history.

In 2005 and 2006, on a different spiritual journey, Archie visited Greece and Turkey to learn more about the apostle Paul and his missionary trips to preach the gospel and spread the word of Jesus. He saw the places where Paul preached, the cities where he stayed. He came to a new level of appreciation of the opposition Paul faced, and what it must have been like for him, how he stood firm in the Word of God without failing.

Visiting the places where Jesus and the apostles spread the Word cemented a level of spiritual learning in Archie that he brought back to his ministry and his congregation. He had always been deeply committed to biblical teaching, and has grown more confident in the power of the Bible and prayer because of his travels.

"The Bible is my Word, which I live by, and I believe it is the true Word of God. Everything God wants from me is laid out in the book, and everything I know I need to be is communicated through prayer. When I'm praying to Him, I'm also communicating with myself, reminding myself to be consistent, obedient, faithful to the Word," said Archie.

The power of prayer is a message Archie delivers regularly to his congregation.

"Prayer stimulates us and activates something within. It pushes us to persist."

Besides travel, Archie's theology has expanded by working regularly with a variety of congregations and serving the community alongside Muslims, Unitarians, Catholics, and Lutherans in Milwaukee.

To Archie, there is more to unite different religions than to divide them. "A religion is a way of doing things," he said. "It's a practice. My religion is about the relationship between me and my Lord. I believe that I'm on the one path to him, and the Christ I believe in was God in the flesh, and my faith tells me that Christ is the path to God. Of course, there are many other religions and I don't judge anyone, but this is the decision I've made for myself, and this is the path I've chosen for my relationship with God."

When Archie prays, he prays in the name of Jesus Christ. In public settings where there may be other religions present, this might rub someone the wrong way, but he doesn't apologize. "You pray from your tradition, and I pray from mine. Who am I to say? I don't try to convert people from other religions and I believe in mutual respect. But I choose to live as a Christian and I don't veer from that."

Part of Archie's Christian theology is recognizing the existence of Satan, which many instill with greater power than he deserves, in Archie's view.

"Satan does no more than God allows him to," believes Archie. "Disease, poverty, and everything bad that has happened is because of greed, rebellion, and sin. Satan might seem to have control, but ultimately it's God who has the power."

Archie believes Satan was an angel who tried to take over and was cast out of heaven. Now, God allows Satan to remain on earth. "Satan's purpose is to keep us confused," says Archie. "He will test us, try to rob us of our salvation, steal from us, and kill us. I have a choice to live God's way or in the way of Satan, and for me there is no choice."

Hell, too, is a place in Archie's mind that contains far greater suffering than that which we suffer on earth. "Hell is a place of weeping and wailing and constant discomfort," he says. "A place where you want to leave but you can't. A place of misery. I have no desire to go there."

Places on earth can be like this, too, Archie recognizes. "We bring so much suffering on ourselves. We make our own heaven and hell on earth, but it doesn't compare to the hell described in the Bible."

Archie strongly believes in the Black Church and the historical role it has played in Black lives. He says during slavery, faith was all that the enslaved had to sustain them and the church was their sanctuary. The church gave the enslaved dignity and assured our forebears that they were loved and equal in the eyes of God; that no matter how unbearable their suffering was, Jesus, who too had suffered, had prepared a place of rest for them when their time was up on earth. It was this religious faith that enabled them to endure their bondage.

The Black church also served as fertile ground to set the stage for emancipation. Nearly every slave rebellion was planned in the Black church. Nat Turner was a minister as was Denmark Vesey and Gabriel Presser. It was in the Black Church where our ancestors planned and prayed for slavery's end.

The Black church offered a culture and salvation outside of the white man's world, and still does so today. While some Black scholars strongly argue that Christianity is the "white man's religion," for Archie, Christianity not only belongs to the Black community at the cultural level, but at the racial level, too.

"Jesus' parents went to Egypt to hide out, and how do you think they managed to blend in? Because they were people of color, that's how. Europeans don't want to acknowledge the truth that civilization started in Africa," said Archie.

"Even today, in most congregations, Europeans have painted Christ and His followers in white skin. "Everyone that's good looks like them," said Archie. "Everyone that's bad looks like us. Once Africans were here in the

Americas, they weren't permitted to practice their own cultures or build their own communities. They were dehumanized and their identities were stolen, their families ruptured, their bodies assaulted and abused. And they were forced to build the country while Europeans took the credit; just like the builders of the pyramids, who worked for the Pharaoh but were not allowed to live inside the walls."

The church, Archie believes, is fundamental to modern Black life. "The church is asked to play so many different roles today. From providing for food banks, to helping members find jobs, from hosting educational classes, to providing counseling services, we play a huge role but we still need Jesus." Religion offers an antidote to that effort to destroy Black culture in this country and elsewhere, Archie believes. "Religion is a way of making something happen. It's about relationships. We must build genuine relationships and share truths."

Part of Archie's theology involves outreach and meeting with church leaders from mostly white communities, like Brookfield and Oconomowoc. His goal is to build bridges between their congregations. But with so much of the region's poverty concentrated in Milwaukee, and so few Black homeowners in the outlying areas, he recognizes that this is a multi-generational struggle. Once, he asked a prominent layperson in a congregation in the suburb of Brookfield, "How could I get your constituents to accept me as a neighbor and an equal?" and the man said, "That would be a problem."

"We are far from done with the work of overcoming fears and phobias," Archie says sadly. "I mentioned to someone who lives out in Hartland that the solution to urban sprawl and redlining is for legislators to pass laws prohibiting these practices and focus on urban housing. A member of a congregation out there said to me, 'That's never going to happen.'"

Many people have their minds made up, Archie knows. "We don't see each other's humanity. And churches are no exception—some of them even spread racism. We can become so blinded that we fail to establish a genuine relationship with God. But if we establish that relationship, we can get along as brothers and sisters. I hope there will come a time when we can ignore skin color and band together as Americans."

Given the current administration in Washington, DC, Archie does not see that happening anytime soon. Archie believes that President Trump represents a significant setback in racial justice and progress.

"He says, 'Make American Great Again,' but he means 'Make America White Again,' while maintaining the system of control. From the very genesis of this country, they have been invested in maintaining their control," he declared about President Trump and people who think like him. "Routinely, the President mobilizes citizens to ignore truth in favor of lies. He does this because of a white fear of losing power and control."

"It's a tragedy that such a person is in office, a person who has verbalized his hatred of women, and non-whites. Obama was in trouble for owning two Blackberries, and this is a guy who's always on Twitter and never shared his taxes."

Archie's theology of outreach led to his involvement in local politics throughout the years. He was appointed by former Democratic Governor James Doyle to be Chair of the Bureau of Milwaukee Child Welfare, where he served for eight years. He's also served on the board of MICAH, a faith-based political group working to improve the lives of poor people in Milwaukee. He's on a first-name basis with the Mayor and the President of the Common Council, and mentors several local politicians. In 2000, the year Al Gore was nominated, he attended the National Democratic Convention in Los Angeles as a delegate.

"But I'm not a Democrat or a Republican—I'm for the people," Archie clarifies.

Some pastors believe it's not right to become involved in politics but Archie disagrees. He believes a spiritual leader has a responsibility to be politically active, to make sure the members of his congregation are registered to vote and are aware of how the proposed policies will affect their everyday lives, even though he does not tell them who to vote for.

Milwaukee has never elected a Black mayor, although four-term Senator Lena Taylor recently ran against Mayor Tom Barrett, primarily on a platform of equal housing opportunity and racial segregation. Unfortunately, she came up short. Notably, the elimination of polling places causing long lines of people waiting hours to vote not only led to voter suppression but exposed these brave people during a Covid-19 pandemic.

"It was bad timing," explains Archie about Taylor's mayoral bid. "Black people have to be almost perfect in our behavior and conduct in order to run for office. Some of the things she's been involved in were stumbling blocks, I fear. She also needs to connect with the whole city of Milwaukee, not just the Black community. The limited voting places certainly didn't help."

That said, Archie feels strongly that his city is behind the times. "Milwaukee is one of the most racist places you'll find."

One way this racism makes itself known is through segregated housing, not only in the city but in the ever-growing suburbs. Even with all of the protests dating back to the 60s, housing choices are still limited in Milwaukee County for Blacks.

Archie recalls the animosity he faced many years ago in Milwaukee. He and Jeanette moved into a little house on 19th Street, and an older white man who lived across the street made a point of making them feel unwelcome, as if their presence were an inconvenience for him. He wasn't going to move, he told Archie, implying that Archie should move instead.

But the Ivy family has experienced welcoming white neighbors, too, including some who shoveled their driveway and cut their grass when they were out of town. Others took a while to warm up but were sincerely sorry to see the family move away.

"Until we can eradicate the system that encourages racism and oppression, we're going to continue to have a big problem in this country," says Archie about the future of Milwaukee and the nation. "Let's not play politics. Let's treat everyone equal as children of God. There is no Black or white—there are just people."

This is the theology that he preaches to his congregation. It's what he said to a couple who came to him for counseling earlier this year, when the discussion turned to how to raise anti-racist children.

"We teach racism from the moment our kids are born into this world, calling people white and Black. Don't call me African American or Black American—call me American."

When asked about one of the most significant events of our time, the Coronavirus that was closing church doors and forcing them to worship online, Archie clarified: "Everyone is panicking now. Maybe we can see this all as a test of our faith. I don't know the purpose but I won't ignore the call. There has always been a plague on mankind, over and over. We'll figure it out, we'll take precautions. God has the answers. He will protect us. Not that I'd put my hand inside a vat of serpents, but I will listen for His guidance."

When Archie is asked to sum up his guiding theology in a nutshell, he returns to the basic principles of his faith: the Father, the Son, and the Holy Spirit.

"God guides me, He identifies me and shows me how to live. He became the flesh in His Son. He came down to experience life the way we experience it, to be in touch with me and the way I live. And because of the sins of Adam, He took up our sins and sacrificed His Son for us. Through Jesus' death, we received salvation and the Holy Spirit remained here to guide us from within. We must live as closely in Christ's image as we can, knowing we'll never be perfect. We will be forgiven, however, through repentance."

God, Archie believes, is a being who cannot be seen but made us in His image, and gave us the ability to think and reason. He's made of love. When Archie talks to children at church about God, he says, "In your own way, can you accept Jesus as one who loves you and cares about you?" He talks to them at their own level. "That's why we have five- and six-years-olds who come forward wanting to be baptized."

Archie believes God created all things including the human race and that He's a loving and forgiving God. "In fact, he loved us so much that he gave His Son for our salvation, and no matter what other message he might offer, this is the crux of it."

As a pastor, Archie feels that his primary responsibility is to God. He believes that he was assigned by God to do the work, to watch over the people, to be an undershepherd to Christ.

"Never to lord over the people, but to serve the people," he added.

To serve in his own way and by living his own life as a model for others, all by the grace of God.

CHAPTER TWELVE
Pastor's Life

<hr>

"Trust in the LORD with all thine heart; and
lean not unto thine own understanding."
–Proverbs 3:5

The life of a pastor is far from simple or peaceful. As Archie will attest, it takes an emotional toll, and the burnout rate for pastors can be very high. This is influenced by the high-stress emotional nature of the work and the need to be constantly available to members of the congregation and the local community.

"You have to be all things to all people," Archie said. "Maybe you have a member who's having a transplant or surgery, and another whose mother is in the hospital, and another who needs you to eulogize her son. All at once."

Pastors are known for not taking enough time for themselves, to renew themselves spiritually and focus on their personal relationships, which leads to family trouble and even divorce. Then, of course, there are the less emotional but still sticky administrative troubles, since most pastors are expected to be their church's CEO as well as spiritual leader.

The church van, for example, comes up a lot in Archie's meetings—who gets to use it, when, and for what purpose. It's just one example of several constant headaches.

"If it's not one thing, it's another," said Archie. "And religious folks are not an easy bunch. I have to be careful. Sometimes when the pressure is on, I take it home with me. When I find myself snapping at my wife, or she reminds me I don't have to use a certain tone of voice, I know I'm letting it get to me," Archie confides.

The pastor must also take on the challenging task of leading people into greater roles in the church organization. This means pastors like Archie are constantly trying to find volunteers to fill important positions in the church, but because they are voluntary positions, some work out better than others.

The pressure on pastors is great, which is why the turnover is so high, higher than most any other profession. Statistics vary, but many studies show that pastors engage in high-stress conflicts with congregants at least once a month, and that many don't earn a livable wage despite working sixty-plus hours a week and taking very little time off.

Children of clergy frequently cite difficult upbringing as the reason they don't attend church as adults, and many studies report high rates of depression and even suicide among clergy. Although not all of these trends apply to Archie directly, he is well aware of the stresses of the job. He vividly recalls a young minister with a wife and two kids who tragically took his own life.

"It's easy to burn yourself out, because you're pulled in so many different directions."

Over the years, Archie has learned to cope with the high stress of being a long-term pastor. One self-preservation tool that he's honed over his years in the ministry is the ability to delegate.

"I try to surround myself with people who are positive and open to learning leadership roles in the church and to get other people involved. You have to invest in growing people," said Archie.

Archie believes in sharing the church leadership instead of shouldering the entire burden. He has no desire to guard the pulpit like it's a sacrilege to share. Once, he spoke to a group of pastors about developing a guidebook for new pastors, offering tips on how to run meetings and set agendas and budgets. "I'd like to put that book in the hand of every one of my congregants," Archie said to the other pastors. They were aghast. Why would he want to do that? Then they would all know as much as he knows. "Exactly," Archie responded to the others. "I want them to know more than I know. I want to give people the mindset that they can be more than they are, to never shackle themselves."

A great leader, Archie believes, nurtures growth in others and puts energy into finding each person's right fit. If a congregant doesn't fit in one team or position, maybe another is better suited.

"I try to find everyone's fit. That way, I don't have to micromanage. That's one way I stay sane," he joked.

One cornerstone of Archie's philosophy toward leadership can be summed up in a sentence: *Agree to disagree but not be disagreeable.*

'I haven't had a disagreement yet that's about the Bible or Scripture. Usually any disagreement that comes up in church is about tradition."

For example, for years the church went to Memphis, Tennessee to fellowship with another congregation there. One year, the church's young people wanted to go on the trip, too, but the adults said they couldn't.

"I felt the young people could and should go on the trip. So, we had a meeting, and one deacon was in support but others were quiet. I asked, 'What's keeping them from going?'

'It's our fellowship,' the adults said. I replied, 'What does the church look like? Doesn't it include our young people too? Have you ever felt alienated and not allowed to participate?'"

The young people were allowed, in the end, to travel for the fellowship, and the event was successful. Archie didn't resolve the problem with an ultimatum or a final word—he resolved it with dialogue, which is usually his first tack when it comes to disagreement.

The pressure of delivering a meaningful message weekly is another challenge of the position. There are highs and lows when it comes to teaching and pastoring. Archie isn't one to think every word he speaks from the pulpit was divinely inspired.

"I never walk away from the pulpit thinking I knocked them dead. I never feel I've done enough, no matter how much I studied and prepared. I've had plenty of sermons that bombed, especially early on."

And what's the goal of a good sermon, according to Archie? A good sermon should be simple, yet extremely ambitious.

"You're hoping to deliver the gospel of Christ to people in a conventional way that will also change their lives."

Pastors are known for never taking a Sabbath, or day off, during the week and working long hours. In an average week—assuming there are no emergencies or crises, which happen more often than not—Archie takes off Monday, the day after the worship service, as a day of self-care.

"That's my day to do what I like. I need a day of rest," he acknowledged. If the weather is nice on a Monday, he'll do something around the house or read or spend time with Jeanette, maybe even go out for breakfast. He schedules no meetings on Mondays, and his staff knows not to task him on that day.

On summer Mondays, he spends time doing one of his favorite recreational activities: golfing. Though most pastors are not surrounded by many friends, since they are typically seen as leaders not equals, Archie stays close with a couple of other pastors who also enjoy golfing. Sometimes they play on a course where pastors golf free—they only pay for the cart—and sometimes they go to various county courses.

"I'm pretty good. My handicap is twenty-four. If I'm under a hundred for eighteen holes, I'm pleased. Usually I hit around ninety-six. Used to be high 80s before surgery, and I'd like to get back there."

The other pastors in his golf group are Walter Harvey, Christopher Boston, Kirk Boyd, and Frank Headd, but Archie is the only senior.

"If I hit from the senior tee, so do they. And if they hit from the blue tee, so do I. I can outdrive most of them, and though I don't come in first all the time, I hold my own. Each year, in the month of February, four of us go on a golfing trip to Orlando, FL, for a fun week of golf."

Also, on Mondays, Archie starts planning for what he intends to preach about the following Sunday.

Tuesday is when the week's cycle starts in earnest. On that day, Archie takes counseling appointments, including premarital counseling or members who need to talk through issues.

"I don't give direct advice, I just listen and ask gentle questions to guide them," he says about counseling. Tuesdays also tend to become busy with other kinds of meetings, as well as his preparation for Bible study on Wednesday.

"The hardest problems I have to deal with are illnesses and death," Archie shares about his counseling. "I don't have a magic wand to wave and make it go away. Lately, I counseled a family who lost a child to murder. I can listen, sure, but I can't take away their pain."

Instead, Archie prays with the members and reads Scripture. He reminds them that God is listening, that He is in tune with their hurt, and because He knows, they can lean on him. He's there for them.

"What can I say? Sometimes I can't find the words, so I pray with them, and I counsel faith and hope."

Archie's message of faith and hope is one he returns to time and again. One recent Sunday, Archie preached on the sustaining power of hope.

"We have the faith and perseverance but hope steadies and sustains us. We know it will get better if we take one step at a time. If you're carrying a heavy load and you can get through one day, you can get through two, then three."

On Wednesdays, Archie spends most of his time and energy on preparing for Bible Study. Sometimes, if he's finished by noon or so, he might have meetings after that. He goes home before Bible study to debrief and spend some time with Jeanette, and then he returns to the church in time to lead a Bible Study group at 6:00 p.m.

Thursday is Archie's day of study. This is when he collects materials, take notes, and puts together the first draft of what will become Sunday's sermon.

"I get my ideas through reading, mostly. Recently I was reading something from 1 Peter about the trials we face, and I wrote in the margin a title for a sermon, then from that, I knew what I was led to talk about that Sunday. *Life is not a problem to be solved but a mystery to be lived.*"

A good sermon, Archie believes, addresses the congregants where they are in the moment, emotionally and spiritually. His sermons aim to engage members intellectually as well as spiritually, to offer truths that they can take away and use in their own lives.

"People are hurting. I don't pray for messages to move people emotionally or excite them or entertain them; I want to help them. I don't get bothered if no one is shouting or waving their hands. I just look for people who are sitting up and listening, and I know I have their attention. I preach about life and living."

"The Lord knows what the end of this day looks like, but we don't. We don't know what's next," said Archie, confirming his fundamental belief that he is doing the work of God.

At this stage, most of the tips and tricks that he valued as a younger pastor have pretty much gone by the wayside, even though they were very useful for him when he was learning and gaining experience. For example, older pastors recommended that he practice his sermons in the mirror before delivering them on Sunday. This helped him figure out what lines to emphasize and which need tweaking, and also how long it will take to deliver the message. "I no longer practice in the mirror, but it was very helpful at the start. By now, I know how long it will take to deliver a sermon."

Archie's typical sermons are thirty minutes to forty-five minutes at the most. When he wants to deliver a broader message, he breaks it into two sermons over two Sundays.

On Friday, Archie continues anything he hasn't finished on Thursday. Then he sits at his computer, writes an outline, and begins to fill it in. He types up all his sermons and has them archived.

On Saturday, Archie attends more church meetings, and if he hasn't quite completed a sermon, he'll add the finishing touches. That night, he prints it out so he has a hard copy, then brings it to the pulpit Sunday morning.

Sunday is the pinnacle of any pastor's long week. Sunday mornings, Archie wakes at 5:30am. He showers and shaves and eats a light breakfast, all while the day's sermon spins around in his mind. At 7:30 a.m., he leaves for church in time for Sunday school to begin, and spends the Sunday school hour walking around the church or meeting with a congregant or staff member.

All morning, he's meditating on the message. "I keep a sign on my door during that time that says 'Do Not Disturb.' Of course, it doesn't work," laughs Archie.

A typical worship service at New Hope starts at 9:30 a.m. First, there's the call to worship, then a litany or song, followed by the reading of the Church's vision statement for the year. Next comes a responsive reading, and then Scripture and prayer. "After prayer, we have a period of praise, we recognize guests, we sing a congregational hymn, and I return with observations." There are three more stages before the sermon: another song from the choir, the offertory, and a reading of Scripture for the sermon.

"My goal is for the service to flow. My minister of music has a lot of input on the order of service and the content."

After the sermon, there's an invitation for new members to join the church, and then a benediction. The service is finished around 11:30 a.m.

Years ago, New Hope held two services every Sunday. This wasn't sustainable for many reasons, not the least of which was the toll it took on Archie. Also, the schedule divided the church into two congregations. Now, with the congregation numbers just shy of 300, everyone is home by noon, allowing for quality time with family after worship.

One of the main responsibilities that weighs heavily on a pastor is the need to constantly raise funds. Archie knows this challenge all too well. Outside of leading people to Christ, money is the biggest challenge of running a church, says Archie. "So many congregants are on fixed incomes, yet so many young people of means who could contribute to the church are not attending."

He encourages tithing and offerings, but he doesn't believe in heavy-handed tactics to force people to give.

"I believe in giving. I don't use gimmicks to entice people, I don't use tricks. I use the biblical principle. When we need to construct a building or fund a program that's needed, I say to the congregation, 'This money is in our pockets.'"

Most of New Hope's members tithe. Last year, the tithing rate went up generously and now the church's budget is just over half a million dollars annually.

"Our financial support comes from the people. We just ask," Archie humbly explains.

In addition to his usual weekly responsibilities, Archie also handles funerals and weddings. He might do two or three funerals in a heavy week. "They come in cycles when you have an older congregation."

Archie considers performing weddings as one of the highlights of being a pastor. He enjoys meeting with couples prior to their wedding. During those meetings, he helps couples discuss what marriage is about and how to make it successful. He often shares tips on overcoming pitfalls that occur in every marriage.

"I do less from the book than from my personal marital experience. I use our history. I tell them, you get out of it what you put into it. We discuss the sacrifices and compromises that will happen in marriages. It's a partnership and a journey, not a contract but a covenant. Forgiveness and most important, love, will help them stay together over time."

Funerals are more challenging, as people grieve differently. So, when he leads funerals, his main goal is to try to help people come to grips with what's happened, with the abrupt change in their lives.

"Some people don't have enough faith and they're torn apart. There's no magic potion to make the pain go away, so I try to speak to the living, to give them hope that God doesn't make mistakes, that before we are born into the world, our time on earth is determined by Him. We have to accept what He allows, and what causes death is sin, not that the victims are sinners, but we are born to live, to die, and to live again," clarified

Archie.

Another important task that Archie leads is implementing the annual church theme. This year, the church's theme is preparing members of the church to serve exceptionally, by equipping them to teach others. Helping people help other people has a ripple effect, Archie believes, and it's a spiritual and personal growth plan. The question Archie asks of the congregants is, what does this plan look like for you as a Christian?

Usually, says Archie, people reply that they don't know. So the church team conducts dialogue and trains them, so they can pass it forward. "I see ministry as equipping people to be more effective in witnessing Christ in our lives and arousing others' curiosity so they will want to do more."

Now that he has so many years under his belt, Archie is mentoring younger pastors. He reminds them to make sure it's not just something they want to do—it must be something they are called to do.

"Just because you want to be a pastor doesn't mean God is calling you. You might get in and then quit. Young pastors tend not to realize everything that's involved with being a pastor," Archie explained solemnly.

For example, shouldering the concerns of the congregation, Archie says, will have you lying awake at night. Many clergy report that seminary didn't prepare them for life in the pulpit, that most of what they know comes from advice from more experienced pastors or from years of learning on the job. Many pastors, too, report that after years of pastoring, their faith can start to weaken, their prayer lives wane, and they feel spiritually undernourished. These are all challenges Archie has fought to overcome throughout his years with New Hope.

"The ministry requires much more than I expected. It requires me to be faithful to God and to people, and I have needed to develop very thick skin. I can't react in the moment. I have to pray for people instead of reacting. I have to let everything roll right off like water on a duck's back, not take it personally."

Similar to anyone in a position of leadership and in the public eye, Archie has fielded his share of criticism. One complaint he's heard a few times is that he treats some people as if they're more special, which he doesn't believe is true.

"Even my wife is just a member when she's here," he states. "Certain people spend more time talking to me, yes, so I know them better. But my door is always open, for anyone."

Another fact that weighs heavily on a pastor's soul is when members—especially valued, long-time members—choose to leave the congregation. Even though it's the congregant's choice, Archie admits he feels the disappointment, especially if he'd thought the relationship was strong and they gave him no warning before leaving.

"One member left because her spouse didn't like something I said at a funeral, for example. That stung. Some of the younger people who encouraged the renovation of our church and helped us get through the initial phase left shortly after. Other people who grew up in the church left after their parents died. Most people don't tell me before they make the move, they just leave. I try not to worry about it, even if it's hard."

Occasionally, too, members might misunderstand something he says from the pulpit or in a meeting, but typically that doesn't result in a serious issue.

Most experienced pastors have considered leaving the pastorate, and Archie is no exception—given the challenges, the attrition, the turnover, and the personality clashes. Time and again, it's his personal conviction that stops him from leaving.

"Despite all of the challenges that I face, I know I'm blessed. I can make decisions, talk out issues, and disagree without losing my temper. I've learned to take time for myself. My wife and I get away. I've learned to adjust and not let things bother me. Sometimes I go home from church, get my golf clubs, and drive to a course not too far from my house. I get a cart and I just swing and meditate in solitude."

"The ministry is lonely," discloses Archie, who has his golfing buddies, his pastor Dr. Fred Crouthers, and his friend Russell Williamson. But he lacks a regular group of ministers to meet with or talk to, except for his good friend, Reverend Carmen Porco.

"My most intimate friendship relationship is in prayer," said Archie.

Taking care of himself is no small thing. A high percentage—as high as seventy percent, some report—of pastors experience depression. Archie believes you have to have a release, and you have to accept that you can't please all people all of the time. "The best you can do is lead by example and build an empowered creative team."

As for running a church, Archie enjoys the preaching much more than the business part. "Management is stressful, whereas preaching is a different kind of stress." Though he works not to let things bother him, he has a few sources of frustration, and one is when people in the congregation don't volunteer. "If you ask people to come forward and they don't, then they're often the first to come forward to criticize. And that's difficult to accept."

Another thing that can wear out a pastor, reflects Archie, is accepting every offer or responding to every problem that comes through the door.

"Identify the two or three things you want to be involved with, and that's it. Otherwise, you can't pastor your own church. I carefully choose organizations where I have relationships and they are doing good things for the community. I serve on a couple of boards, and that's enough."

Pastors' children also bear the brunt of the life chosen by their parents. Archie observed that when his kids were small, people seemed to expect them to act like they were older than they were, as if they weren't still children.

More was expected of them. Yet from his kids' perspective, they sometimes felt neglected by their dad, who gave so much of his attention to other children in the congregation.

Growth, Archie believes, is New Hope's greatest challenge. Archie can't avoid talking about attrition in the congregation, which is due to a number of factors, including death and members moving. "We always need a plan for bringing in new members," says Archie.

"If we had all 300 members attending, it would be okay, but some Sundays, we have less than 200 at the service. If we had 500, that would be super. We're working to increase the numbers. We have evangelistic Sunday every third Sunday. If we could have more parking closer to the building, that would help, I believe. We're looking into that long-term. Church growth isn't just about numbers of people, but also about members attending consistently."

That said, the numbers alone don't make a strong church, and Archie is well aware of the need for balance. If higher numbers are all a pastor seeks, there might be a loss in the intimacy of the community, and the warmth and comfort offered there.

"We want our people to be received like family," he explained. "It's less about how many people belong but about their attitudes and hearts."

Yet New Hope must engage in recruiting new members, or it will lose the next generation of potential congregants, Archie fears.

"The millennials are a different breed," he observes. "They're not going to accept the status quo. Churches everywhere are waning in membership whether they are Catholic, Lutheran, or Baptist. It's different pastoring in the southern states than in Wisconsin. There, the churches are filled with people, but that's not true here."

Archie believes that people are drifting away from the church's purpose, away from the respect that society has held, historically, for the church. He recalls that his grandmother told him that Christianity was branching into so many sects, offering so many differing messages, that people were losing their way. The answer, he posits, is to dig deep into the true history of Christianity.

"I'm preparing to teach a class on the history of the African American church, and I'm learning some things about how religion was used to control people and keep them in their place. But the church was also used to liberate Black people. I believe that there's a God, and I want my kids and grandkids to see Him as He is through the lens of history."

When people tell Archie that they don't believe in God but they do believe in some higher power, Archie's response is: "That is God." He tells them to open their minds, to remember that the Bible might not be new but it's still relevant. "God doesn't change," he says, "He's the same forever. There are biblical truths that are relevant now and then and always."

CHAPTER THIRTEEN
Church Is Community

"The LORD is my strength and my shield; my heart trusted in him, and I am helped: therefore my heart greatly rejoiceth; and with my song will I praise him." –Psalms 28:7

The Black Church has always played a vital role in the community. In fact, it would be impossible to think of the Black community without thinking of the Black Church. After slavery, freed Blacks established churches apart from their former masters. These new churches created communities and worship practices that were culturally distinct and relevant.

From the beginning, the Black Church has not only spoken to the spiritual needs of Blacks but has acted as a first responder to their social, economic, and cultural needs as well. Black churches have established schools during reconstruction, provided for the indigent, and led the fight for social and economic justice. Black churches played critical roles during the civil rights movement. It's no accident that most of the leaders of the movement were preachers. Black preachers spoke truth to power, encouraged education and economic growth, and were often the primary link between the Black and white communities.

Today, deep social problems resulting from institutional inequities plague every central city in America. The Black Church is in the center of fashioning a response to the scourge of drugs, gangs, violent crime, unemployment, and other social ills.

New Hope Missionary Baptist Church is continuing the long tradition of service the Black Church is known for. It is located in Milwaukee's African American community on Roosevelt Drive. One look at its Sunday Worship Program and you soon get a pretty clear picture of how vested New Hope is in the community. There are announcements on scholarships, a leadership summit, bake sale, sick and shut-in report, prayer and spiritual enrichment, and food banks, to name a few. It has multiple ministries such as its Adult/Family Ministry and Youth and Children's Ministry.

Archie believes he has a mandate from the Bible to be involved in the community because the New Testament is replete with instructions for Christians to care for the least, the lost, and the left behind. "We are Christ's disciples. We know that Jesus fed the hungry and healed the sick."

He recognizes that too many of Milwaukee's Black citizens are without. They're without good healthcare. They're without good homes. They're without a good school system. They're without jobs that pay a livable wage. Too often the Black Church is the only institution they can turn to in times of need. The church is the only institution that Black people in this country have ever continuously owned and managed.

Poverty causes hopelessness and anger. People in the central city, almost daily, take their anger out on each other leading to violence and death, especially among young Black males. And when this infighting results in death, like it does in every major city in the U.S., it is the Black church that performs these tragic funerals and often has to raise the money to help families cover funeral expenses.

A church is a community resource, believes Archie. If someone comes to him in need, for food or a handout, he believes the church has a duty to help if possible.

"Man, a pastor has to deal with a lot of different issues. For example, if one of my members said, 'Pastor, they're about to turn off my lights,' I need to be able to direct her so she can get the help she needs." The church doesn't have the resources to provide a safety net for all the folks who need help, Archie acknowledges. He adds that you have to discern who is panhandling and who is seriously needy, but the church can serve as a resource and a referral site. "The church must help people advocate for themselves. If we can help them find the resources they need, they may soon be able to walk on their own."

The church is in a unique position to know what its community needs. "It's more than us feeling good on Sunday morning. The Black Church must get work done Monday through Saturday. Then we can come to church on Sunday and celebrate. We have enormous work that needs to be done in our communities. This work allows us to build our faith muscles and watch the Holy Spirit come alive in our neighborhoods. If there was ever a time that we needed the church to let its light shine, that time is now."

Prior to Archie becoming the pastor of New Hope, the church already had many strong programs in place and was active in Milwaukee's central city. There was a great music ministry, for one thing, including six choirs. There was even a radio broadcast back in the day, under Pastor Lathem's leadership.

"New Hope has always been a fellowshipping church," says Archie. "We coordinate fellowship with other churches."

However, after he was on the job for a while, he noticed that there had been a reduction in outreach activities, which he believes was primarily the result of an aging congregation. Also, he observed how hard people were having to work in their roles, given the variety and number of various church programs.

"We downsized," he firmly disclosed. For example, the church went from six choirs to four: a sanctuary choir, a mass choir, a men's choir, and a youth choir. These choirs alternate singing in the main worship service, and often, they are invited to sing elsewhere in the community.

New Hope is known today for its powerful evangelical component, as well as for equipping and exalting its members and the community, for its strong Christian education program, and for strengthening families and impacting the community in many positive ways.

"We're friendly, loving, welcoming, and we have structure. We're organized and we work together," Archie boasts of his church.

As only the second pastor that New Hope has ever had, Archie sees his placement there as ordained by God.

"This is the Lord's place," he says. "I'm here by assignment. I was delivered here by Him."

His approach to New Hope, when he became their pastor, was that the job wasn't about him, or him alone—it was about the church as a whole, what they could accomplish together.

"That was always my attitude—the place is about us, not me."

At Christian Union, Archie's first pastoral placement, he'd tried to spread a message of encouraging leadership and growing the church, less about numbers than strength and commitment. Good leadership, Archie believes, emphasizes authenticity in one's commitment to Christ, and living by example, not only at church but also in the home.

"I believe I've taught our church members by example how to treat their spouses and families and how to build a positive relationship with God as well as fulfill their commitments to themselves and their neighbors."

New Hope has twice launched a Spiritual Gift inventory, to match members of the congregation with ways to help. "There's no such thing as a pew member—everyone who worships here needs to be involved in the ministry, even if it's just making phone calls. Every designated ministry has an assistant they're training to replace themselves. If you're willing to be trained, you can be, and then you can take someone by the hand. We rotate our ministry leaders. After six years, the assistant steps up. We train so many people to be leaders that it makes for a powerful organization."

Above all, Archie's message to his congregation is that the church represents the body of Christ, that together all members function as a group, sharing their gifts and working to support and reach out to others. Together, they can help each other find a way to a better life, to find joy despite sorrow, to feel hope. "New Hope, when everyone works together, can be a powerful resource for the wider community, through evangelizing, equipping and exalting others, and extending itself to those in need."

"It's no small task to encourage people to get serious about their commitment to Christ. Not to religion, but to Christ." Archie believes people need to be more dutiful about carrying out the mandate of witnessing, teaching, and being an example in their communities.

"I'm not talking about in the church building, but in the whole community, and in their own homes. We've adapted a lifestyle that is contrary to God. The building is not the church. The individuals who gather here are the church."

When there's confusion, uncertainty, or controversy, Archie can always find reliable guidance in the Bible. He doesn't care about being politically correct, and believes that if Jesus was political, maybe he is, too.

"Some pastors don't take that stand, but you have to be political to challenge anyone on an issue, you have to take a side. The church is political, not partisan."

God has given us free will, Archie believes, and it's our responsibility to use that free will to emulate Him. "We make choices like Adam in the garden; we're not robots. God's not a starter and a stopper of events."

This doesn't mean God doesn't care, however. We can't understand the mind of God, says Archie, but we must accept His will. The choices we make have consequences.

Recently, Archie participated in the establishment of Milwaukee's Urban Center, a religious organization that held a consultation bringing church and city leaders together to explore the role the church should play in tackling social ills in the community. The pastors and community leaders discussed the church's power to address Black community needs. Many concluded that the church either does not believe in its power or understand its power or maybe a combination of both. They felt that the church needs to leverage its power in strategic ways to benefit the Black community.

The faith community is embedded in the Black community and in Archie's eyes, must be engaged in the solutions to the problems its congregants are facing. "If we're not, why would people want to attend a church that won't address any of the issues that they're facing?" Archie asks. "When I look out at my congregation on Sundays, I see myself. That's why I understand their reality. I see the despair but I also see tremendous possibilities if we are able submit to God's will."

Archie concluded with the admonition that serving others is at the heart of the ministry of Jesus.

"We must see our involvement in community as central to what it means to be church!"

Archie says when he sits at the table with city leaders and decision makers, he's there not for himself but for other people. Isn't that the true meaning of community?

CHAPTER FOURTEEN
Testimony From Friends

"Cast thy burden upon the LORD, and he shall sustain thee: he shall never suffer the righteous to be moved." –Psalm 55:22

Dr. Howard Fuller has known Archie for more than twenty-five years, dating back to a time when Dr. Fuller's mother attended New Hope as a member of the congregation. However, even before knowing Archie through New Hope, Dr. Fuller was the Superintendent of Milwaukee Public Schools when Archie was a principal. After they first met in the educational arena, Fuller needed a new, effective principal at North Division High School, and so he pulled Archie from South Division High to fill the role. He did this for three reasons, he said: "Archie's professionalism, personality, and relationships with the community."

"I knew him personally, so that helped, but the job was a tough one. It worked out, I'm happy to say," added Fuller.

Fuller has known a number of leaders in his time in education, and he draws a distinction between loud leaders and quiet ones. "Reverend Ivy is in the quiet category," he explained. "He's not an in-your-face person but he's still effective. He gets things done, but then afterward, you might not even realize he was involved, because he's not the type to seek credit."

Leading a church as a senior pastor is a job that takes any number of skill sets and personality traits, which Fuller recognizes as one of the reasons Archie was so well-suited to the job.

"Being pastor of a church is one of the most political jobs in America," Fuller explains. "It's a business to a certain extent, and you can't have the buildings if you don't have money, so you have to keep growing from a business standpoint and from a faith standpoint. A pastor has to be a father, grandfather, brother, teacher, and counselor. A pastor has to be able to soothe people and talk them down from a ledge and keep the congregation together and help it grow at the same time."

New Hope is a testament to Archie's talents in all of these arenas. Above all that, Pastor Ivy is Fuller's personal friend and confidante, one of the few people he feels he can trust with his own private problems. Like anyone, Fuller has experienced his fair share of personal and professional challenges, and Archie has always offered counsel and prayer.

"He's one of my go-to people," shared Fuller, "and I try to be that for him as well."

Together with other community leaders, Archie and Howard founded the Clergy for Educational Options (CEO) Leadership Academy in 2004, the result of years of work based on the thorny Milwaukee School Choice program that passed in 1989 and expanded to include religious schools in 1995. The original school started in Archie's church, New Hope, then outgrew the space and moved into its own space in 2007. In 2011, its board of directors decided to become a charter school to widen the school's public appeal. They removed religion from the curriculum and changed the name of the school to Commitment Excellence and Opportunity Leadership

Academy. Most people didn't notice the change, since its initials were still CEO.

Over the past fifteen years, Archie has remained a crucial voice on the school's board and only original pastor to remain involved. Recently, following an enhanced mission statement to prepare young scholars for college, the school was renamed Milwaukee Collegiate Academy, and last year Dr. Fuller's name was added to honor his lifetime commitment to education. Today, the Dr. Howard Fuller Collegiate Academy is thriving in its own building on 29th Street in Milwaukee. The Academy boasts a one-hundred-percent college acceptance rate over the past seven years. The class of 2020 earned more than $3.5 million in scholarship dollars. Over 330 students are enrolled in the high school.

The school is tangible proof of Archie's deep and effective commitment to making changes in the lives of underrepresented communities. Another example, added Fuller, is his leadership of New Hope.

"When you look at the mere fact that New Hope exists, that Reverend Ivy has sustained this institution in the Black community, and that it's vibrant and thriving, that's a remarkable fact on its face."

A pastor must keep his flock, preach the gospel, attract younger people—and the competition is fierce, though no one wants to put it that way, of course.

"Some churches survive and some don't," said Fuller.

Fuller's principle concern these days is that Archie has a tendency to work himself too hard and take on too much responsibility.

"The burden of being both a pastor and a leader in the community is a heavy weight," he explained, speaking from experience about his own workload.

"People can be all kinds of things," Fuller stated, "including fickle and unreliable and self-aggrandizing." Archie always does what he says he'll do, as does Fuller, and there's a deep mutual respect and love between them born from their lifelong, individual commitment to being authentic.

Fuller hopes that Archie uses this book opportunity, about his work and life, to tell his own story in his own words, and take ownership of his contributions as a pastor, a leader, a husband, a father, and a grandfather.

"This is a chance to put himself on the record. Without that, you're at the mercy of other people's interpretations of you. They'll do that anyway, but if you write your own book, you have a say."

"The bottom line," said Fuller, "is that Archie is a genuinely good man whose strengths outnumber his weaknesses, and has lived a good life. You can see the mutual love between us," he said.

Cory Nettles has known Archie for more than twenty years, since Cory was a member of the youth Baptist Convention with New Hope. Today, Cory is the President of Generation Growth Capital, Inc., but he first met Archie when Archie was being vetted for the pastorship at New Hope.

"My initial impression, way back then, was that he was a servant leader with a big heart for missionary work and for our community. You could tell right away that he'd spent his life as an educator."

Shortly after Archie came to New Hope, he shared a vision for what's now known as the Triangle of Hope Ministry, an expansion of the physical church to include a school and wellness center. Cory could see this vision clearly and stepped up to help convey the vision to parishioners, to rally support, and ultimately to help execute the expansion.

"Through that experience, I saw how hard it was for a servant leader to bring a vision to people who are skeptical. He had to convince the louder minority voices and the naysayers. But through his own leadership he was able to overcome and build excitement for his vision and see larger portions of the vision realized."

Archie loves a good laugh, Cory says, and doesn't take himself too seriously. On Pastor Appreciation Day, for example, there's always a lot of joking and teasing, and some of the deacons are pretty sharp with their barbs, but Archie always takes it in stride.

"I have so many memories of him preaching sermons, filled with the Spirit and beating his head or ruffling his hair, back when he had more of it. He's a good-natured, good-humored guy, who never takes anything too personally."

Like Archie, Cory is accustomed to being the one to whom people turn to with their problems. Once or twice, Archie has told Cory that he's concerned that Cory needs to slow down, maybe take a break. Cory thinks this is a welcome change since most people typically approach him with a new task or request for additional help.

"He has the ability to zero in on me, as I'm sure he does with everyone else, and show genuine concern and compassion. I also consider him a big cheerleader. Very seldom is there recognition for me or my wife that he doesn't find out about and wish us well. He's rooting for us personally, and that means a lot," reflected Cory.

Cory remembers Reverend Lathem, Archie's predecessor, and respects the work Archie did to step into the long shadow the man left behind. "Archie never tried to overshadow Lathem's legacy, and he was always his own person, humbly making his own legacy."

"For someone to have that kind of security in the context of a Baptist church where there had been this iconic leader before you, for him to have the agency to step into that role as the second pastor ever, spoke volumes about him."

Cory's wife sits on the board, along with Archie, of the Dr. Howard Fuller Collegiate Academy, a choice school for predominantly Black kids, out of her passion around urban education.

"The school is a significant part of Pastor Ivy's legacy," says Cory. "To have a school run by Black people for Black people; that is Black-led and high performing, is without precedent in Milwaukee."

Cory regards Archie as a close friend, a good Christian who works to model Christian values and behavior, and a self-aware man who knows he's fallible and subject to error. "At a time where leadership is in short supply, particularly African American male leadership, he's trying to live out in his own way the values that Christ instructs of us."

Rev. Fred Crouthers has known Archie more than thirty years and has stories about his friend he wouldn't dare share. But really, he describes Archie as a man of great integrity and impeccable character—a close personal friend.

Rev. Crouthers and Archie met for the first time back in the 1970s, when the Baptist convention had an extension seminary and ministerial group of non-pastors who worked together. Archie's pastor had recommended him—he was a member of Providence at the time—so even though Fred had heard of Archie, this was the first time they met. Archie wasn't yet a pastor but Fred was.

"Some people come into your life and they remain," reflected Fred. "Archie is a person who has been with me over the years, and we share similar ideas and character. We even worked through our Masters and Doctorate degrees together. He's a good person to bounce ideas off of. But if you're looking not for the truth, but for someone to make you feel good, he'd be the wrong person for that."

Back in Seminary, Fred recalls that Archie was known as "The Brain," because he could solve a work problem in a blink and bail out his fellow students by rephrasing the professor's questions in a clearer way. At New Hope, Fred has observed that Archie can resolve differing opinions by helping people understand ideas in new ways, just like he did back in seminary.

What sets Archie apart, according to Fred, other than his terrific sense of humor, is that he combines two styles of preaching: the intellectual and the charismatic.

"He has a great personality. He's warm, people take to him quickly, and he communicates well with people on all levels."

Archie is a leader, says Fred, and will be the first one to step up to any request made of his congregation. He's also a great supporter of other pastors, their drives and anniversaries, and the first to offer assistance.

"He's counseled a number of younger pastors and they've enthusiastically joined his congregation."

———

Rev. Dr. Russell Williamson is the Pastor at Zion Hill Missionary Baptist Church in Milwaukee and has known Archie since 1978. They met in what used to be called the Minister's Union, but got to know each other when Archie first became a deacon. Russell had been a deacon himself, and his church had visited Archie's in fellowship. They became more acquainted during their Minister's Union State Convention.

Russell's first impression of Archie was that he was a little laid back and reserved, a serious individual. "His preaching style is unique," Russell explains. "He's not the average African American preacher, hollering and that kind of thing. He reads Scripture and goes deep into it instead of preaching on the surface. He makes it simple enough that the average individual can understand his message."

Plus, Russell says, he's fun to be around. He has a sense of humor and can laugh about a lot of things.

"Sometimes I crack him up with my jokes, but then he's also just a well-rounded individual. Someone used the term that he's the kind of fellow who can walk with kings and never lose the common touch."

A few years ago, Russell had a heart attack, and it moves him now to recollect how Archie came to his side. He was the go-to friend who made sure he was following the medical advice, and Russell put his life in Archie's hands.

"The contributions Archie has made to his church and community are nothing short of excellent," says Russell. He'll leave a legacy that everything he came into contact with, he made better. Once you get to know him, you love him. Just the way he carries himself."

———————

Rev. Dr. Demetrius K. Williams has preached several times over the years at New Hope since returning to his hometown of Milwaukee, after Hurricane Katrina in 2005. Archie opened doors that made Rev. Williams' transition from New Orleans back to Milwaukee smoother and full of opportunities, a fact for which Williams continues to be grateful to this day.

Much like everyone who knows Archie, Williams also says Archie is committed to his family and to the church. He also acknowledges Archie's integrity and leadership.

"Dr. Ivy's intentional and visionary leadership has inspired stability for his congregation," said Williams. "He never just waves and say hello. He mingles at the various tables, greets and fellowships with the people. I have found him to be a "people person."

———————

Rev. Joseph H. Jackson, Jr., first met Archie on Mother's Day of 1982, thirty-eight years ago. "Immediately, I was taken to him by his welcome and spiritual glow," declared Jackson.

In Jackson's words, Archie became his "pusher man," which means that it was Archie who encouraged Jackson into leadership positions in Sunday School and the Boy Scouts, and into becoming Youth Director. "He pushed me beyond my comfort zone."

The two men had more in common than was apparent at first glance. Like Archie, Jackson also struggled to accept and announce his call to higher ministry. One afternoon, Jackson recalled, he was pacing in front of the Senior Pastor's door, hesitant to knock. This went on for several minutes, until Archie emerged from the sanctuary and said to Jackson, "Go ahead, get it off you!" They didn't speak more in that moment, but Jackson was reassured by Archie's intuitive understanding of his struggle.

Later, Archie would push Jackson again into the position of President of MICAH, and he and his family would support Jackson as he raised two kids as a single parent. Jeanette would become a spiritual guide for Jackson as well.

"Rev. Ivy is God's man. An imperfect man striving for perfection," described Jackson admiringly.

Rev. Joseph W. Ellwanger has known Archie since the early 1990s, when he brought the New Hope congregation into MICAH. Ellwanger's first impressions of Archie were extremely positive. Right away, he could tell Archie was friendly, serious about education of Milwaukee's underserved kids, and a generous leader.

"Once I called him on his cell phone about a MICAH Religious Leaders meeting coming up, asking him to fill a role on the agenda," recalled Ellwanger. "He said he couldn't give me a firm answer until he got back to the office to check his calendar, because at the moment he was on the golf course. He wouldn't be able to get back to me until late that afternoon or the next day."

The conversation told Ellwanger everything he needed to know about Archie—that he knew how to take care of himself and take time off, which would serve an important role in his long-term outlook as a pastor. And that he trusted Ellwanger as a colleague, to give out his private number and answer his calls, even during his free time.

"From that point on, I knew that he was truly committed to the justice work of MICAH," he said.

Moreover, Ellwanger's experience as a white pastor working in racial justice has instilled in him a particular respect for people like Archie, who can work effectively across denomination lines and across racial lines.

"He has been more of a colleague to me than many pastors in my own denomination."

It's Archie's personal spiritual strength, Ellwanger believes, as well as his outward-looking stance on life, as a person and as a pastor that made it possible for him to make such a positive impact on so many people in Milwaukee and beyond.

"Instead of being a self-centered person, he is an other-centered person. Instead of focusing only on building his own congregation and 'fiefdom,' he has been willing to become engaged in the larger community, in congregation-based organizing, and in justice work. As a result, he paradoxically, made a name for himself."

───────

Rev. Terry J. West, Sr., met Archie in 2002, when he first started visiting New Hope as a congregant.

"There was an immediate bonding between us which led to my becoming a member of the church," he reflected about Archie.

Today, Rev. West is an Associate Minister at New Hope, after sixteen years as a member, serving under Archie's tutelage. In West's experience, Archie's strength is that he lives the life that he preaches about daily, never asking his members to do anything he doesn't do himself. "A model Christian, he lives by God's word and believes that God takes care of His own."

"Recently, the members walked into our church building and the sanctuary was cold because the heat wasn't on," said West. "Pastor Ivy announced that we will not allow the enemy to still our joy. Go get your coats and put them on. We are trusting that God will take care of us, so let's praise God anyway. After about ten minutes the heat came back on and the rest is history!"

Over the years, Archie has invited West to become a part of his immediate family, like a brother. The bond has lasted over time, and when West underwent bypass surgery, Archie started a practice of checking in on him that continues to this day.

West wants people to understand that Pastor Ivy is a man of his word, gives faithfully without hesitation, at home and at church, and is a man after God's own heart. Under Archie's leadership, every voice matters. Archie's been academically and biblically trained to lead.

"He is the same Pastor Ivy every day. Amen!" exclaimed West.

Rev. Dr. Dennis Jacobsen, a retired ELCA Lutheran pastor, has known Archie for thirty years. Like most people who know him, Jacobsen saw immediately that Archie was an influential pastor and a natural leader. But there was more to him, Jacobsen soon realized. One day, they met in Archie's office to discuss a MICAH issue, and Archie was deliberating how to bring the issue to the attention of the governor, with whom he had a personal relationship.

"Then, in the course of the meeting, Rev. Ivy shifted the conversation to include discussion of how each of us was dealing with the emotional burdens and challenges we were facing in our respective roles as parish pastors. Rev. Ivy has a strong capacity to be relational even when addressing public arena issues. He is both pastoral and prophetic," said Jacobsen.

Archie has influenced Jacobsen over the years to practice self-care, and Jacobsen has offered him the same. In the world of organizing, it's common for leaders to drive themselves and others too hard in pursuit of justice, Jacobsen explained.

"Rev. Ivy has always stressed the need for balance. He walks the walk. And he does so with integrity and deep devotion to God and neighbor. He is an educator who has much to offer intellectually and conceptually with insights rooted in personal experience. Rev. Ivy is an ideal servant-leader."

Rev. Carmen Porco has known Archie for six years or so. They met through the Housing Ministries of Wisconsin, of which Carmen is the CEO. Archie was a potential board member, who was to replace the retiring Rev. Roy Nabors—an iconic former Milwaukee pastor and leader. On first meeting, Carmen discovered Archie had an impressive ability to listen to the board's challenges and sort out the dynamics of the housing program's various issues.

"He's very analytical and is able to clarify the issue, ethics, and integrity-to-mission statement. I was impressed with his depth of discipleship and not the usual Christian language of judgment and isolation of those that are different."

Through the board's trials, Archie continued to prove himself a gentle comrade and smart thinker, never undermining Carmen's position and backing him up as needed.

"Archie has rekindled my faith in the institutional church by showing his style of leadership and deep focus on teaching his flock about discipleship. He doesn't wear his religion on his sleeve; it comes out of the spirit of his soul and he walks the talk, day in and day out. This has been an inspiration to me on matters of faith and social justice."

What comes to mind when Carmen thinks of Archie's passion for justice is that he is constantly jogging people out of the complacency that develops over time in a city like Milwaukee.

"He makes a difference by being the different drummer that keeps the beat to the silent majority who want to make a difference."

Carmen regards Archie as a consummate theologian. "He practices what he preaches and preaches the worth of all and the covenant of God to redeem the most hateful because of the unconditional love that is at the center of divinity. He is a man who has suffered the very oppressions that we think are of a bygone era that are alive today and oppress millions into subservience and silence. He has endured the suffering that makes one an effective servant of God trying to fulfill the Kingdom of God on earth. He answers his calling with the devotion of being a servant and places himself in the position to make a difference."

"He knows suffering and as one who has suffered, he knows how to see the sorrow of the soul and tunnels into the person with grace and redemptive effect. He has helped me though the loss of my wife to cancer. Unlike most ministers that are only with you for the moment, Archie continues to minister long after such an event. He is authentic in being human and yet carrying out the divine imperative to love your neighbors as yourself."

Mose Ivy, Archie's youngest brother moved to Milwaukee in the mid-80s, primarily because he needed a new start. "I had gone through a divorce in Mississippi and had reached rock-bottom," he shares. "Archie gave me a place to recover. I stayed with him for about six months until I could get on my feet."

When Mose thinks about growing up in Shannon, Mississippi, he recalls that it was a rough time in his life. He says that Archie, as the oldest kid, was the leader of the family when his dad was gone. "I remember those ass-whippings he used to give me when I screwed up. I was a pretty rough kid. Even though I didn't think I needed those whippings back then, looking back, I can see where I could have used even more guidance as a kid," he admits. "I remember my mom telling me if I got into trouble, she would put Archie on me. Archie loved us, but he wouldn't hesitate to keep us in line and follow my mom's directions."

There were stark differences between Archie's path and Mose's. "I didn't get the education that Archie did. I felt I was pushed out of school. I was a pretty good athlete; baseball was my thing, although I played football and basketball. But education wasn't my main focus."

When asked about his brother's influence on the Ivy family, Mose does not hesitate. "Archie has always supported our family. He helped me personally and he helped our mom. He's probably helped everyone in our family. If something happened, he would always come home, no matter where he was, to be with the family. He still checks on me and gives me guidance. I respect my brother totally."

Mose said for years, people in Milwaukee didn't even know they were brothers. "I live in a different part of town than he does and we run in different circles. I never heard anyone say a negative thing about him. In fact, some of my friends had Archie as a shop teacher back in the day. And they tell me how he impacted their lives. They say he's a good, quiet man, and he helped them do this or that."

Mose says a lot of people don't know that Archie has a great sense of humor. "He's a jokester! He'll cut you up pretty good."

Mose says his brother loves his family and his church and "I love him!"

CHAPTER FIFTEEN

Reflections

---

*"The LORD shall fight for you, and ye shall
hold your peace."* –Exodus 14:14

Archie spent his childhood in the Deep South during the heyday of
the Klan, as well as the normalization of Colored and White signs in
restaurants, hotels, bathrooms, and above water fountains. There was separate
seating on the buses with Blacks forced to sit in the far back. And, he
recalls most vividly and with the most intense regret, "separate but equal"
education. Which meant in reality, that school was not equal at all, especially
for Black kids like him.

"We knew that at certain places, the front door was for white folks and
the back door was for us," recalled Archie. "I guess that's why I've fought so
hard for education all these years. I never want any Black kid to have to go
in the back door. We belong at the front of the line."

Three years ago, Archie told his life story in front of an audience during a
Black History program at New Hope Missionary Baptist Church, where he
serves as pastor. He explained how he'd grown up the oldest of ten children,
with heavy responsibilities at home throughout his childhood, and how he

was held back and told he'd never amount to anything—and there he was that day, telling the members of the audience his central message, which came directly from his own father: *Never let others define who you become.*

He also relayed one other of the few pieces of direct advice he received from his father: *Never say you can't. Always say you can*; and that's what Archie has done throughout his life. Despite the odds, he has persevered and will leave a legacy his family can be proud of. He learned early on to control his temper and to let his actions speak for him.

He shared a story about his interaction with Hal Burgess when he was home from college one summer. Burgess, was a white man who owned the dairy barn where Archie worked in high school. He asked Archie to draw up a schematic for a new dairy barn using what he'd learned in his engineering classes. This was the same man who'd once asked Archie why the coloreds wanted to go to school with white folks, since Blacks had their own schools, second-rate as they were. This was also the same man who told a young Archie he knew a surefire way to plan the assassinations of both President John F. Kennedy and Dr. Martin Luther King, Jr. This profound violent disclosure, spoken in such a matter-of-fact way, showed Archie, the true soul of Mr. Burgess.

In response to a racist like Hal Burgess, who never expressed any humility or reluctance to speak out against the rights of Blacks, Archie held his tongue and didn't debate the issue. He had been taught to be slow to speak but quick to listen, how to act instead of reacting. He prided himself from a young age on never showing disrespect, even when disrespect was being shown to him. He also understood the consequences of what could happen to him, if he didn't hold his tongue. Holding one's tongue doesn't mean silence, it means knowing when to speak and choosing the right words. The self-control he learned by growing up in the South among outspoken racists helped him survive, no doubt.

"Being around people like Hal Burgess, I learned that no matter how they treat you to your face, deep down, they are always going to be who they really are. When you worked for Burgess, he paid you and his wife cooked you lunch. On the surface, it may have seemed that things were normal. But in reality, his racism went deep, and to him I was never anything close to being an equal."

A few years later, having graduated from college and becoming a teacher in the Milwaukee Public Schools, Archie would return to Hal Burgess' dairy barn driving a 1967 Buick Grand Sport 400, a car he'd purchased on his own. "I knew you would make it," grimaced Burgess to Archie at that time.

"I don't think his heart had really changed," Archie reflected, "but he had to see that God had blessed me."

When Archie reflects on his long and productive life, he can honestly say that he has valued faith, family, and community above all else. For three decades, he has shared his time and energy, his vision for the future, and his leadership skills with his New Hope congregation. It is clear that without his influence, New Hope would not be the community it is today, and many of its congregants would not have found their paths toward God.

By teaching and by example, Archie has demonstrated what it means to be a servant and a leader. He's modeled how to overcome challenges and live by the word of God. His children are living proof that their father's message persists, as they each define themselves and their lives in the same way that Archie does.

"I believe I've offered an example of how to live in a godly way," he said. "Day or night, I'm consistent. When you encounter me, you always encounter the same person."

In the future, when Archie is called home to God, he believes he will be welcomed as a good and faithful servant. For Archie, life has not always gone as planned, but it has unfolded according to God's will, and retirement is no exception.

"I thought I'd be done pastoring by now, but my calling doesn't have an end date," he said. "I might step down from the pulpit, but I'll never turn away from my calling to serve."

As for regrets, Archie can't deny he's suffered some disappointments and setbacks. He wishes he'd had a closer relationship with his father. It still pains him that he was held back in school as a child, and how that one decision affected his sense of security and belonging for so many years. It still pains him to think of what was missing from his childhood, too, the biking around with friends and living carefree, without the responsibilities of many younger siblings.

But Archie won't revisit the past without recognizing that the twists and turns in his life's journey delivered him to where he is today.

"Regrets are life lessons," he said, and then repeated one of his enduring mantras: "Life is not a problem to be solved but a mystery to be lived."

The timing of a person's life and calling, Archie believes, is in God's hands. From experience he knows there is only so much a person can do to resist God's plan. He looks back on his own struggle to accept the calling and wishes it could have gone more smoothly, with less pain in his own heart. Archie believes that even with God in charge, a person must command his own future, not only by rejecting bitterness in favor of self-determination, but also by setting personal goals and working to reach them.

"How we respond to His Will impacts our future," he said. "I've felt bitterness, sure, but the crucial thing is how I've responded. Hopefully in a way that respects God's Will."

To his children and grandchildren, he offers the example of his life, a strong set of ideals, and some practical advice.

"Get something in your hands that no one can take from you, no matter what setbacks occur. Get an education. Learn how to look people in the eye and learn how to give respect and earn it. If you do that, you'll be able to accept any challenge He sends your way."

Archie plans to step down in his role as Senior Pastor at New Hope Baptist Church within the next few years. He's working now to ensure a smooth transition once he finally relinquishes the pastorship. A smooth transition will make all the difference between an institution that continues to thrive and grow, and one that loses momentum. He intends to leave his church stronger and more resilient than when he found it. His legacy, no doubt will include a renovated space that matches his original vision, with teaching, worship, and shared space, and a stronger commitment to the health and wellbeing of the surrounding community.

When Archie casts his eye toward the future of The New Hope Baptist Church, his greatest wish is that the Triangle of Hope 501C3, that the church has established under his leadership, will continue to be a place where people are helped, housed, and educated, where families come together and children feel safe and flourish. The Triangle of Hope is a nonprofit cooperation established in 2004. The future plans are to develop the three other properties, creating housing, a family wellness center, and a medical clinic.

"Already, the changes we've made are impacting the lives of families in the community, making them better," beams Archie proudly. "My greatest wish is that we'll be here in the Garden Homes community well into the future, as a place of hope for our neighbors."

Will he consider moving back to Shannon, Mississippi, once he retires? For a time, Archie considered buying more land in his hometown and maybe raising cattle. But eventually, he gave up this dream because of practical reasons.

Archie's brother, Joe, who endured two tours (1966-1970) in Vietnam came back from the war like many soldiers—out of sorts. So he decided to return home to Shannon.

Archie bought Joe a two-acre parcel of land there, as a loan. Joe didn't live long enough to repay the loan because he died from complications from Agent Orange in 2008. Archie finally sold the land in January 2020.

"Who would take care of the land while I was up north?" Archie asked himself. He would have to completely depend on others, which isn't his strong suit. Also, there's no major airport; the nearest hospital is in Tupelo, about ten miles north of Shannon, resources Archie and his wife will likely require in their later years. For now, Archie has reconciled himself to never live again in Shannon, the place that meant so much to him and shaped him into the man he's become.

"I like rural living. It's great to spread out. I've fantasized about having ten acres with a fishing pond, but at this stage in my life, that's not what I need."

Plus, the Shannon of his childhood with his great extended family and sense of community, no longer exists. When he takes his grandkids down to meet the cousins who have remained there, he shows them the town and the school he attended. His old high school is now an integrated elementary school, the kind he didn't attend because of Mississippi's racist segregation laws. Although the Shannon he grew up in has changed, many of the wounds caused by racism still remain.

But his roots are there and his religious underpinnings began in a little church that nurtured him and prepared him for a life of service. He remembers fondly all of the activities that the church provided for young people and longs for that sense of community to exist throughout the nation.

For Archie, the meaning of life can be found in the Bible. He believes Christians should remain faithful and truthful while having personal goals and a plan to accomplish those goals. He believes in aiming high, and that you live your best life each day because tomorrow is not promised. "What comes around the corner, we don't know," he says. "Each day offers challenges and choices. However, faith-based people must remain hopeful."

"I can always look forward for tomorrow being better than today," he declared.

For the country, Archie admits that these are dark times, with a President who brags about the economy even as wages of low earners stagnate, or are lost entirely. While corporations expand their wealth, said Archie, low earners can't make ends meet. What's the answer? It's complex but there are a few places to start: "educating generations about institutional racism; shoring up and fully protecting voter rights; and developing our economy with less dependence on China for low wages and cheap goods."

"We need to get back in this country to depending on ourselves. I'd like to see America become a place where there's no sunset on voter rights, where if you're a citizen of this country, you're treated equally, and your rights are the same as everyone else's," he declared.

For his adopted hometown, Milwaukee, where he has worked his entire adult life, Archie hopes that racism will cease to exist someday, that the place will eventually become a city for all people. He hopes communities will stabilize and the violence will stop.

"When will we as a people stop killing each other?" he asks mournfully. "When I first came here, the Black community in Milwaukee was a place of peace. You could trust people and raise a family without feeling threatened. My hope is that this again becomes a city without bars on the windows and doors, where people feel safe."

For his children, Archie hopes that they will maintain their closeness to each other, as family, and that they will walk in step with the Lord despite any obstacles thrown in their paths. He hopes they will be consistent in their relationship with God. He also hopes that his own example and life lessons will be passed down to future generations and that people are inspired by his story.

"My hope is that we continue to walk together as brothers and sisters in Christ, for the cause of God. I hope that he will receive the glory of everything we do. It's His world; He left us in charge of it, and I hate to think we're messing it up every time He turns around," he added.

Archie is proud of his religious community and still dreams for a different future, one in which skin color no longer determines who has the power and who doesn't. But for now, he says, on Sunday morning, the most segregated place in the world is still the church.

Archie prays that whoever replaces him behind the pulpit will work with the people of New Hope, and build on the foundation that he has laid. "I have tried to fight the good fight and to live my life in a way that people know I'm a man of God. All praise goes to Jesus who placed me here by assignment."

APPENDIX A

Awards and Acknowledgements

COMMUNITY:

Outstanding and Dedicated Service Award; Central City Organization, 1977 & 1979.

Athletes For Youth (AFY); Loyal Support and Development of Youth, 1972-1979.

Board Member CEO, 2001

Federal Bureau of Investigation (F.B. I.); Citizen's Academy Award, 2002.

Heritage Registry; Who's Who, 2004.

Founding Member: Jackson State University Alumni Chapter; Milwaukee Chapter, 2005.

Black Excellence Award, 2006.

MICAH'S Community Leadership Award, 2008

Milwaukee Police Department (MPD) Citizen's Academy Award, 2010.

MICAH'S, Do What Is Just; Justice Legacy Award, 2011.

Bureau of Milwaukee Child Welfare, Dedicated Service Award, 2011

Milwaukee Community Journal; Contribution Towards Making Our Community Stronger Award, 2013.

Jackson State University, Milwaukee Alumni Chapter; Trailblazer Award 2018.

EDUCATION:

MPS – High School Principals Assn; Outstanding Leadership and Dedicated Service Award, 1997.

Milwaukee Public Schools (MPS) Outstanding 30 years' Service Award, 1997.

MMABSE Conference Retiree 30-year Service Award, 1997.

State Superintendent's Friend of Education Award, 2005.

African American Heritage; Outstanding Education Award, 2006.

Milwaukee Collegiate Academy (MCA) Dedicated Service Award, 2018.

OMEGA PSI PHI FRATERNITY INC. KAPPA PHI CHAPTER:

25-year Service Award, 1993.

Founders Day Speaker Award, 1997.

Scholarship Award, 2006.

Outstanding Community Leader and Christian Leader Award, 2006.

Lifetime Achievement Award, 2016.

50-year Service Award, 2018.

RELIGION:

Proclamations; numerous proclamations 1989 through 2020.

Certificates of Appreciation; numerous certificates of appreciation 1989 -2020.

Wisconsin General Baptist State Convention Service Award, 2011.

Wisconsin Baptist Laymen Movement; Outstanding Community Service Award, 2019.

APPENDIX B
Sample Sermons

GOD'S GLORY, OUR COMFORT
("Some Things Worth Shouting About")
(Isaiah 40:3-8)

We are in the duel season of football and basketball, where in the state of Wisconsin there are sports teams that are exciting to watch, at the collegiate level and the professional level. How many of you get excited just watching on TV, not to mention attending a game? At games there is a lot of cheering and shouting, very few are yawning. Folks are excited and not afraid to let anyone know about it. They are screaming, cheering, and shouting!

In this passage before us, we find some issues that are exciting, that are worth shouting about because they are exciting or because they are serious matters. This second Sunday of advent we will focus our attention on three issues that surface in this portion of Scripture that are worth shouting about. The first thing worth shouting about is:

I.   THE ARRIVAL OF THE SAVIOR IS WORTH SHOUTING (Isaiah 40:3-5).

"The voice of one crying in the wilderness: Prepare the way of the LORD; Make straight in the desert a highway for our God... Every valley shall be exalted and every mountain and hill brought low; the crooked places shall be made straight, and the rough places smooth; the glory of the LORD shall be revealed. And all flesh shall see it together; for the mouth of the LORD has spoken" (NKJV).

By Divine providence and revelation, Isaiah looked into the future and saw the arrival of the Lord Jesus Christ into this world. The word recorded in Mark 1:1-3, parallels the words of Isaiah 40:3-5, regarding the ministry of John the Baptist preparing the way for the ministry of Jesus.

"The beginning of the gospel of Jesus Christ, the Son of God; *As it is written in the prophets; Behold, I send My messenger before your face, which shall prepare your way before you. The voice of one crying in the wilderness: prepare the way of the LORD; make His paths straight"*

The cry of the voice in verses 3-5 is a cry of wonderful news: prepare the way for the LORD, for He is soon coming. This is a picture of the Near East custom of sending ambassadors ahead of the king to announce His coming. A king's visit to an area was a cause for great celebration. Enormous preparations would be made. Either a special road would be built or an existing roadway would be upgraded and readied for the king's appearance. Preparations always included leveling the roadway by filling in the valleys, lowering the hills, and straightening out the crooked sections. All obstacles that lay in the roadway would be removed.

With the LORD'S announced coming, the people were to make the most careful preparations. They were to:

- *Straighten out their lives and remove all crooked unrighteous behavior.*
- *Level out the paths of their lives: be consistent, obedient, and faithful, riding smoothly over all the valleys hill, and mountains, the ups and downs of life, with confident and righteous behavior.*

180

The promise to those who prepared for the Lord's coming. God's glory would be revealed to them (v.5). All mankind would see His glory... John is the forerunner of the Lord Jesus Christ. He was the voice crying in the wilderness preparing the way for the coming of Christ. But in reality, this prophecy applies to every human being in every generation... We all must prepare for the coming of the Lord... In Isaiah's day the Jews needed to prepare for the Lord's coming to deliver them from Babylonian captivity... In John's day the people needed to prepare by doing exactly what he preached; repent and be baptized, for the Lamb of God who takes away the sins of the world was soon coming... Today, people need to prepare by staying alert and watching for the Lord's return... We must be thoughtful, living righteous, godly lives, looking for the blessed hope and glorious appearing of the great God, the Lord and Savior Jesus Christ.

The glory of Christ was revealed when He was on earth. His glory was revealed in His virgin birth, in His sinless life, in the healing of the sick, the feeding of the hungry, the raising of the dead, His love for mankind, His death on the cross, and His resurrection from the grave... We serve a risen Savior! This is the glorious message of the Gospel! Christ paid the ultimate price for the sins of mankind. Yet, He is alive! I would say, that's worth shouting about!

Not only is the arrival of the Savior worth shouting about:

II.   THE SHORTNESS OF YOUR LIFE NEEDS TO BE SHOUTED.

"The voice said, "Cry out! And he said, "What shall I cry?" All flesh is grass; and all its loveliness is like the flower of the field. The grass withers, the flower fades, because the breath of the Lord blows upon it; surely people are grass" (Isaiah 40:6-7).

The instructions of the voice in the wilderness was to cry or shout out. Notice what was to be the subject of the shout. Man is like grass that withers away and his kindness or goodness is like fading flowers. In other words, we are here and then we are gone. We fade quickly. It is said that the average man lives 74 years. That is 888 months, 3,884 weeks, 27,010 days, 648,240 hours and 38,894,400 minutes, or just over two billion heart beats. But, when compared to eternity, that's not very much!

The shortness of our lives is to be shouted as a warning because there are some very important decisions we must make before our life on this side ends. The matter of the brevity of life is repeated throughout the Bible. As he sat in ashes, suffering excruciating pain form his nauseating disease, Job pondered the briefness of life in:

- **Job 7:6-9 (NLT)** – *"My days fly faster than a weaver's shuttle. They end without hope... O God, remember that my life is but a breath, and I will never again feel happiness... You see me now, but not for long. You will look for me, but I will be gone... Just as a cloud dissipates and vanishes, those who die will not come back."*

- **Job 8:9 (NLT)** - *"For we were born but yesterday and know nothing. Our days on earth are as fleeting as a shadow."*

- **Job 9:25 (NLT)** – *"Now my days are swifter than a post: they flee away, they see no good."*

- **Job 14:1-2 (NLT)** – *"How frail is humanity! How short is life, how full of trouble! We blossom like a flower and then wither. Like a passing shadow, we quickly disappear."*

James informs us in chapter 4:14:

- **(NKJV)** – *"Whereas you know not what shall be on tomorrow. For what is your life? It is even as a vapor, that appears for a little while, and then vanishes away."*

— **(NLT)** – *"How do you know what your life will be like tomorrow? Your life is like the morning fog – it's here a little while, then it's gone."*

The word "appears" comes from the Greek word phaino *(fah '-ee-no)* which means "to shine as to attract." Life might be full of show, glitter, noise, boasting, and activity, but then it's soon over. The glitter will not matter then. Only what you have done for the Lord and with the Lord will be important… We are quick to count our years at each birthday; but God tells us to "number our days." Make our days count for Christ! In Psalm 90:12 we find these words: *"So teach us to number our days, that we may apply our hearts unto wisdom."*

The shortness of our lives is to be shouted! Why, you may ask? Because eternity is only a heartbeat away from any of us. You may wake up in your bed in the morning but be in the morgue by midnight… That may be a little gruesome for you, but some of us need to be shaken out of fantasy-land life and confronted with reality!

Eternity is forever and the decision one makes about Jesus Christ today will have eternal consequences. Heaven is for real and so is Hell. The grave is not the end, it is the doorway to one of two destines; a lake or a mansion… For those without a relationship with Jesus Christ, will spend eternity in the Lake of Fire… For those who have placed their faith in Jesus Christ for salvation, will enjoy eternal life in a place prepared for them (John 14:2).

So far, we have examined two issues in the text worth shouting about:

- The arrival of the Savior is worth shouting about.
- The shortness of Your Life needs to be shouted.

The next thing to shout is:

III. THE DURABABILITY OF THE SRCIPTURE IS TO BE SHOUTED.

Isaiah 4:8 (NKJV) – *"The grass withers, the flower fades; but the Word of our God stands forever."*

Whereas human life is ever so short compared to eternity, God and His Word stand forever--"shout" it. Yes, people age, deteriorate, fail, and die, but God's promises in His Word are eternal: sure, enduring, lasting forever--"Shout it…" The Word of God is imperishable, never withers, or fades. As born-again Christians, we must believe in the Word of God. We must believe that it is the inspired Word of God. We must believe that it is absolutely without error. We must believe that when the Word of God speaks, we must listen. What we believe it influences how we behave, and it is the message we proclaim. The Word of God is a source of strength that enable us to cope with the trials and circumstances that we are faced with day by day.

The grass withers, the flower fades, but the Word of our God stands forever. The Word of God will be fulfilled, proven, verified through all the years of time, and also of eternity… Consequently, as people of God, Israelites could trust the durability of God's Word. It didn't matter how hopeless their situation or circumstances seemed, it is far from being hopeless. They could have great hope in the future, for God will fulfill His promises… Will deliver His people from their captivity, their oppressors, and their hardships… The great Savior is coming when the people of God will be set free… No matter what they are facing, the people of God, those who truly trust Him and His Word, will be set free.

- *"For verily I say unto you, "Till heaven and earth pass away, one jot or one tittle shall in no wise pass from the law, till all be fulfilled"* (**Mat. 5:18**).

- *"Heaven and earth shall pass away: but My Words shall not pass away"* (**Luke 21:33**).

The urgent and practical question for us is, what can we do to quicken the coming of the Lord in His redeeming and regenerating power:

1. Fill up the gulfs of unbelief; let not lack of faith on the part of anyone hinder the putting forth of Divine power.

2. Remove the hills of inconsistency; let not profession and exhortation be neutralized by immoralities in life and living, by wide departure from the will and Word of God.

3. Take up the stones of blemish; make a patient effort to cast aside lesser evils which, of not serious obstacles, do yet trouble and impede.

4. Lay down a highway by prayer and zeal.

Therefore, beloved of the Lord, we can shout of the arrival of the Savior: "For God so-loved the world that He gave His only begotten Son... The Son was born, lived, here thirty-three years... Died, was buried, and rose with all power... Shout!

Shout that man that is born of a woman is but a few days, and full of trouble. Yes, life is short, but there is eternal life after this life! Shout and thank God for eternal life through Jesus Christ. And shout, and thank God for the durability of His Word!

FROM THE PIT TO THE PINNACLE OF PRIASE
(HOW TO GO FROM A SAD SITUATION TO JUBILENT PRAISE)
(Psalm 40:1-3)

As we explore the words of the text before us, I would like to pose a question to someone here today. Have you ever been in a pit in life? I don't have to tell you what it's like... When you're in a pit there is a sense of hopelessness and helplessness, a sense of utter despair that can be so powerful that it's easy to believe there is no way out....

Whether it is from the pain of rejection, the sting of betrayal, loneliness in your relationship, the ache of financial struggle, harassing health issues, or even the loss of a job, or a dream, which causes one to begin sinking down into a dark slimy pit. Before long you're wondering if you'll ever be able to crawl back out... The question for us to ponder and to give serious thought to is this; can you be patient in a pit under pressure?

We all go through trials, situations, and circumstances in life and living. Being a Christian does not exempt us from the trials of life. Trials are used as instruments to test and perfect our faith.

It was when he was in trouble that David cried out to God for help, even though the answer was slow in coming. His faith in God enabled him to remain patient until help arrived... "From the horrible pit to the pinnacle of praise," going from your lowest point in life to the highest point of praise; in the words of this text we have the benefits of having confidence in God.

Jesus is our Supreme example of patience under pressure, He was in the Garden of Gethsemane as He prayed, He was patience when He was on trial before His accusers, and even on the Cross He was patient... Charles Spurgeon makes the claim; "Job in his ash pit does not equal Jesus on the cross."

When you find yourself in the pit, remember no pit is impenetrable to a God who specializes in pulling His people from the slimiest of pits. I don't know what your pit is; maybe your pit is a destructive relationship that is keeping you down, or a habit that has developed into a hardship... Your pit could be repeated disappointments that seem unbearable... I would also say that, most of the time those of us who struggle with feeling like we're in a pit already have a relationship with God, but we're struggling to live victoriously.... And we're wondering at times, if God cares to deliver us one more time.

Try as you may, you will never successfully pull yourself out of a pit... The characteristics of a pit are stiff mud and mire... It is the kind of muck and mire that doesn't allow traction for your feet. It's stiff, sticky and you're stuck... And as much as you'd like to, as self-sufficient as you'd like to be, you can't pull yourself out alone, and someone else has to come to your rescue... When your struggle to get out of your pit appears to have entrenched you deeper in your pit, shout out to God! You can go from the pit to the pinnacle of praise if you remember:

I. WHEN WE ARE SINKING SEEK GOD (VV. 1-2).

"I waited patiently for the Lord; and He inclined unto me, and heard my cry."

There is a Divine law of waiting which has an essential connection with a larger law of giving. From the deepest depth, the faintest whisper of true prayer will reach the throne of God, and will be responded to by God. Notice, what the psalmist says; *"I waited patiently for the LORD."* Literally, meaning, "In waiting I waited." He continued to wait for the interposition of God... Many of our prayers are not answered because we do not wait for an answer, and do not expect an answer... David persevered in prayer; he waited expecting the succor and salvation of God... That salvation did not come quickly; but he patiently waited, believing, hoping, praying, and expecting it to come.

- In waiting for God, we discover our distance from Him.
- Waiting fosters the sense of a need which God alone can satisfy.
- Waiting shows, us the importance of an open confession of God.

Patient waiting for the Lord is quite consistent with boldness in design and promptitude in action, and is only inconsistent with the unbelieving...

"I waited patiently for the Lord; and He inclined unto me, and heard my cry."

"And He inclined unto me, and heard my cry." The word inclined in Hebrew is *natah (naw-taw)*, and it means to bend away, there is a variety of applications to this word (i.e. to carry aside, deliver, and go down, outstretched, to take aside, and to turn aside)... Here it means I got God's attention, because in the very next breath David says, "And he heard my cry.

We can be sure that God is aware of our need, nothing escapes God's view nor takes Him by surprise, and we may think He doesn't care, but He is there and He cares. Someone said He was there all the time."

Jesus says in Luke 19:10; *"For the Son of Man has come to seek and to save that which was lost."*

"He brought me up also out of a horrible pit, out of the miry clay, and set my feet upon a rock, and established my going" (verse 2).

At this point in his life David felt as if he was sunk in deep and dark depression, he was what we would describe as "down," had been brought very low, plunged into great despondency and despair... We know very well what brings us into the pit--situations of life. Grief can do it, failure and a multiplicity of other things can create pits for us. Times of darkness doom and gloom and isolation from the world... But above all this, it is sin that takes the "lift" and buoyancy out of life and makes it the victim of an appalling gravitation, which sucks it into abysmal depths of helplessness and darkness and despair...

In this horrible pit in which David had sunk, nothing is heard except the howling of wild beasts, or the hollow sounds of the winds reverberating from the broken craggy sides of the roof.

When we are sinking seek God. He will lift you out of your pit; *"He brought me out of a horrible pit, out of the miry clay, and set my feet upon a rock…"* The muck, mud and miry clay, I was stuck in a pit of miry clay; where the longer I stayed the deeper I sank, and was utterly unable to save myself… I was in a place called the "pit of perdition, the miry clay of hopelessness, and the mud of corruption." These are figurative expressions to point out to us the dreary, dismal, ruinous state of sin and guilt, and the utter inability of a condemned sinner to save him/herself either from the guilt of their conscience, or the corruption of their heart…

Jesus knows about the pit of miry clay, He waits for the call of the one's sinking; He will answer and lift them up… And He will do it right on time…. He will change your state from guilt to pardon, from corruption to holiness… God not only will bring you out, David said; He placed my feet upon a rock and brought purpose to my life. He will do the same for you and me. He is the same God… I was sinking deep in sin, far from the peaceful shore…

II. WHEN WE HAVE BEEN SAVED FROM OUR PIT, GOD GIVES US A NEW SONG (vv. 2-3).

"And set my feet upon a rock, and established my going. And He hath put a new song in my mouth, even praise unto our God." Cheerfulness and joy had long been a stranger to David, but now he had a firm foundation to stand on. His directions in life were established and given new meaning. The Lord had given a new occasion for praise, and by filling David's heart with grateful gladness, had given him the disposition to offer fresh praise unto Him… Salvation is a joyous, a blessed thing… It tunes one's heart with music, and the world with beauty and song. ***"He hath put a new song in my mouth…***

This was joy-inspiring; I can now sing "trouble don't last always." This new song:

- It is not a sorrowful song.
- It is a song of praise.
- It is praise for answered prayer.
- It is a praise song for being lifted out of the horrible pit.
- It is praise for escaping the miry clay.
- It is a song of praise for being set on the solid rock.
- It is praise for a new life built on the promises of God.

III. WHEN WE START PRAISING, PEOPLE START PRAYING (v.3b).

"Even praise unto our God: many shall see it, and fear, and shall trust in the Lord." The doings of God in the life of His people are manifested and is influential; Praising saints make praying sinners:

- Praising proves the reality of our faith.
- Praising demonstrates the power of God's love, mercy and grace.

"Many shall see and fear and shall trust in the Lord." When a person is converted the change in their lives is visible, and will command reverence. "Many shall see, and fear." So, when others see you celebrating the blessing of God in life and living. When others see divine grace at work in your life, they too will seek that grace for their own lives; they will be encouraged to trust Him also:

- Those in the pit of miry clay want to be lifted to safety.
- They want something solid on which to build their lives.
- They long to place their feet on the solid rock.

Pouting Christians are poor representatives of their Lord: Praising Christians are missionaries wherever they go…

The question is; have you been lifted from the pit of sin? Has Jesus filled your heart with a new song of joy? If so prepare to welcome others into the fellowship of praise!

Oh, praise Him! Jesus Christ is the Solid Rock on which the lost sinking soul can find solid footing, where God has given steadfast hope. He expects that there should be a steady, regular walk and conduct… Just as God filled David's heart with joy, as well as peace and there was a ripple effect, many saw and feared and put their trust in God…. He will do the same for you this day. He will lift you from your horrible pit, place you on a rock, put a new song in your mouth, and there will be a ripple effect also. Others will see it and reference (fear) and will trust Him! So today let everything that has breath praise the Lord!

Praise Him!!!

Praise Him!!!

Praise Him!!!

He is the great pit picker upper!!!

HOPEFUL PATIENCE

"For we are safe in this hope, but hope that is seen is not hope; for why does one still hope for what is seen? But if we hope for what we do not see, we eagerly wait for it with perseverance"
(Romans 8:24-25 NKJV).

Christians, like the rest of the creation, waits for full redemption, both consciously and aspiringly. As Christians we are heirs who have not yet entered into the possession of our inheritance. We are saved from the guilt of sin, and are released from its power. Our sun is veiled under the morning clouds, and we shall soon rejoice in cloudless splendor… The believer's state of hope is the condition in which and the instrument by which they work out their complete salvation. Let us notice in the text three things about "hopeful patience:

I.   HOPE IS EXERCISED ON THE UNSEEN

Hope is defined as: assured expectation, confident knowledge, inward possession, spiritual surety. The hope of the believer cannot be defined as the world defines hope. The hope of the believer is entirely different from the world's hope or desire or wish. The world desires and wishes for what it can see, and they may or may not be able to get what they long for. The believer's hope is entirely different in that it deals with the spiritual things and the believer will unquestionably get what is hoped for…

("Now faith is the substance of things hoped for, the evidence of things not seen" (Heb. 11:1). The believer's hope is based on the inward experience and the witness of God's Spirit. The believer knows that the Spirit of God lives in them and they actually experience the things of the Spirit now. Granted, the experience is but a taste; the things of the Spirit are not yet perfected in the life of the believer, but they do exist, and they are present in the body of the believer.

We can say with assurance that the believer already possesses the things of God while in the flesh. The believer's hope of salvation is a present experience, he/she is saved now, already has a taste of salvation. Hope for the believer is a living reality now; therefore, their hope is a sure hope. For the genuine believer, hope is the absolute assurance of things promised, but not yet seen (cf. Heb. 11:1). "For we are saved in this hope, but hope that is seen is not hope; for why does one still hope for what is seen" (Rom. 8:24)?

What we see is directly before us; what we hope for is still in the future. Hope is faith written in the future. One could say that it is the invisible womb of time, and there is absolute assurance because we already experience the things of God; they are already an inward possession, a spiritual surety, and outward expectation, a confident knowledge.

You see, God has chosen for us to be saved by hope and not by sight; *("hope that is seen is not hope; for why does one still hope for what is seen" (Rom. 8 24:b)*? If we were saved by sight, we would not hope in God. If we could actually see and experience perfect redemption and salvation now, then there would be nothing more for which to hope for... The results would be catastrophic: we would not be drawing close to God, believing and trusting Him, nor looking to Him to provide a perfect salvation for us... There would be no liberty and freedom between God and man, no love and trust established... There just would be no relationship and no fellowship between man and God, not based on a free moral love, trust, and belief.

Faith and hope are inseparable companions; where faith is, hope is near. Hope is faith in the attitude of looking toward better things to come. It vividly pictures the approaching glory, and is "the present enjoyment of future good." The Christian hope is not a mirage that mocks the mind, but is surely grounded on the work of the Lord Jesus Christ, who has revealed the character of God and His far reaching purpose of love. Many are depending on high expectations has found them baseless; the legacy is absent, the coveted post is given to another. When the skeptic speaks of "a bird in the hand being preferable to two in the bush," we can reply that by the very nature of the case Christian anticipation is precluded from being satisfied with the temporal. "We look for a new heaven and a new earth."

Hopeful patience--hope is not only seen in the unseen, but also:

II. HOPE DRIVES OUT DESPAIR, THE FOE OF PATIENCE

The text says; *"we are saved in this hope."* Hope saves us, for it is hope that keeps us seeking after God and His redemption... We hope for redemption; therefore, *"with patience we wait for it."* Patience; longsuffering, forebear, to undergo trials with joy and anticipation; waiting for fully overcoming; therefore, we eagerly wait! This is being "hopeful patient." "We hope" (v. 25) and "we wait." In verses 23 and 25 we have the words "eagerly" and "patiently." These two words give us a picture of what "hopeful patience" looks like:

1. Hope is one of the great words of the Christian vocabulary;

    a. "Blessed hope" (Titus 2:13).

    b. "The hope of glory" (Col. 1:27).

    c. One of the three virtues; "These three remain: faith, hope and love" (1 Cor. 13:13).

    d. In Romans 5: 3-5, Paul writes; *"We know that the suffering produces perseverance; perseverance, character; and character, hope. And hope does not disappoint us, because God has poured out His love in our hearts by the Holy Spirit, whom He has given us."*

2. The word hope has two senses: (1) an attitude of hopefulness, and (2) the content of that which we hope. Both uses of the word occur in the text, the idea of content in verse 24 ("in this hope we are saved") and attitude of hopefulness in verses 24 and 25 ("we hope").

3. We wait. More specifically, we wait for them, which is the second verb Paul uses. Verse 23 says; "We wait eagerly." Verse 25 says; "We wait patiently." It is important to take the two adverbs together, because Biblical "patience" is not passivity. It's active, and patient waiting expresses itself in vigorous service for Christ even while we wait for His appearing.

God is after one thing; our being patient in hope, that is, our persevering hope. Why you may ask? Because the more we hope for salvation and redemption, the closer we draw to God. And, above all else, God wants us to draw near to Him; fellowshipping, believing, trusting, loving, and hoping in Him.

"Draw near to Me, and I will draw near to you."

The path of hope is the only way God could choose for salvation. It is only as one hopes in God will they draw near to God; and in reality, the more one hopes in God, the closer they are drawn to God... The more one hopes, the more they will trust, believe, love and depend upon God. And this is exactly what God is after; it is His plan and purpose for man and His world.

Where despondency grows, there activity ceases. What this means is that life has been quenched because the light of hope has vanished first? The gospel, by its promise of a free pardon for the penitent sinner, rolls away the burden from the back, enables the criminal to take heart of grace, and to exchange the dungeon of dreary fate for the glad sunlight of a new lease of endeavor after righteousness. There is a danger of succumbing to the weariness of the long Christian journey, but hope grasps the future and draws us to it... Hopeful in the Pilgrim,' Progress,' had much to do to keep his brother above the water; but he confronted him saying, "Brother, I see the gate, men standing by to receive us." Notice the words of this *poem*:

"Hope, like the glimmering taper's light,

Adorns and cheers the way;

And still, as darker grows the night,

Emits a brighter ray."

As believers we are not as shipwrecked mariners, uncertain, if any vessels will pass near enough to save us; we know, if we wait patiently, "He that comes will come, and will not tarry."

Hopeful patience is not only seen in the unseen and drives out despair, it develops the desire for patience:

IV. HOPE FITS THE SOUL FOR ITS FUTURE ARENA OF GLORY.

For every state job, certain qualifications are required. Similarly if we want to play a part in an event, there are requirement that must be met. Preparation must be made. And in all cases waiting is a part of the process. The necessary waiting is a beneficial discipline testing perseverance and faithfulness. The disciple of Jesus Christ can abstain from worldly indulgences because of more cherished longings. He will not barter away his birthright even though he is faced with hunger… "Every man that has this hope in him purifies himself." Yes, hope is the great engine of progress and reformation…

Hopeful patience, is a confident, deliverance hope. It is a hope that brings salvation… *"We are saved in this hope"* (v. 24a), that is our salvation is the source and cause of our hope… When a person is saved, they come into a great hope where they formerly had none… Salvation brings to the believer hope that the world can never give…

Hopeful patience is a defining hope (v. 24b); *"But hope that is seen is not hope; but what a man sees, why does he yet hope for?"* This hope is not visible, something realized… It is yet to come… This hope says, there is more in store for the redeemed than what they already have… If you already have something, you don't hope for that something.

Hopeful patience is the hope of duration; *"But if we hope for what we do not see, we eagerly wait for it with perseverance"* (v. 25) … The greatness of this hope increases the patience in waiting, the greatness of the hope gives the believer more patience to endure adversity from living a godly life... Hopeful patience allows God to develop us (cf. Isaiah 40:31).

HOW TO DEFEAT YOUR BITTERNESS
(When Life Is Out Of Place Part 5)
Luke 15:25-32

Have you ever felt that you have been mistreated? We all have, and our natural reaction is to become angry and bitter. When you become bitter, you get off the path of living Godly. Once you're off the path, then the "thorn" of a past offense festers, when you refuse to allow the Lord to remove it.

In the story of the prodigal son, much attention is given to the son running away from home and returning to his father. Yet, the tail end of this story is like a sandy beach speckled with covered dimes, nickels, and quarters that people have dropped while playing in the sand. It is rich in treasures for us to apply to our lives. Some may have preferred that this story end with the prodigal being restored by his father, yet there are valuable lessons to be learned by the response of the elder brother. The elder brother, like many of us, has a problem with the sin of bitterness. Bitterness is strong feelings of hatred, anger, cynicism, and resentment toward someone because of a real or imagined wrong.

Before we explore this lesson, let's look at who this elder is in this story. He certainly represents the Pharisees who resented Christ's interest in sinners (cf. Luke 15:2). Among us ,the elder brother represents those who, in self-conceit think they are good enough to live in the Father's home, and have not need of being "found," or made "alive again." To them soul-winning activities are most distasteful. It is hard for them to realize that our self-righteousness is but filthy rags of a prodigal in the sight of God.

If you are here today, and if your life is out of place because of bitterness, there are three requirements in the text for dealing with the sin of bitterness.

I. ANALYZE THE CAUSE OF YOUR BITTERNESS (LUKE 15:25-28A).

"Now his older brother was in the field. And as he came and drew near to the house, he heard music and dancing... So he called one of the servants and asked what do these things mean... And he said to him, "Your brother has come, and because he has received him safe and sound, your father has killed the fatted calf... "But he was angry and would not go in."

In our last lesson, the prodigal son has just returned home and is being joyfully received, and welcomed by his loving father (vss. 20-24). As we analyze the response of the elder brother to the return of his younger brother critical insights are gained. When he returned from the field, this means he was attending the duties of the estate. The elder son, unlike the prodigal son, was a faithful worker and a good steward of his inheritance. As he nears the house, he hears music and dancing (v. 25), but he cannot believe what he is hearing. So, he called one of the servants as to what is going on, and is informed that his brother had returned home, and because he has returned safe and sound, your father has killed the fatted calf. His father and some of the servants are celebrating (v. 26-27).

Instead of being happy that his brother had returned home, "he became angry and would not go inside." In other words he developed a "Not Fair" Syndrome. He thought within himself, I am the one who has remained home working in the fields and being faithful to my father. While on the other hand, his prodigal younger brother has caused his father worry, pain, grief, and even shame by squandering his inheritance in riotous living. Totally unfair. We all have felt this way at one time or another and can relate to him very well. If the truth is told, most of us are just like the elder brother, we have felt the sting of incidents that are unfair...

When anger boils over it causes bitterness to rise up as it did in the elder brother in Luke 15:28a; *"But he was angry and would not go in."* Bitterness is caused by anger... There are three causes of anger: (1) hurt, (2) frustration, and (3) fear (fear that someone will take someone or something from you). All three are involved in the older son's anger. He is frustrated because

199

his faithfulness to his father seem to be unrewarded. He is hurt and fearful the younger brother will take his place with the father. So, he begins to "fret," (HARA, har-raw) the word means burning anger that boils over and becomes bitterness. Bitterness always originates with anger. Therefore, analyze the cause of your bitterness and then:

II. REALIZE THE CONSEQUENCES OF YOUR BITTERNESS (LUKE 15:28B-30).

"Therefore, his father came out and pleaded with him" (15:28b). The father leaves the celebration, comes out and pleads with his older son to join the celebration. However, the son's replies: *"Lo, these many years I have been serving you; I never transgressed your commandment at any time; and yet you never gave me a young goat, that I might make merry with my friends" (15:29)*. Bitter people, like the older brother, are always filled with pride and arrogance about their own goodness. Notice the words of Proverbs 8:13a-b; *"The fear of the Lord is to hate evil; Pride and arrogance and the evil way."*

Because of his pride and arrogance, the older son can see all kinds of wrong in his younger brother and in his father. Therefore, in 15:30, notice what he says to his father; *"But as soon as this son of yours came, who has devoured your living with harlots you killed the fatted calf for him."* Bitterness always spreads because a bitter person is never bitter towards just one person but towards anyone who is nice to that person. Therefore, the older son is now bitter toward his father. He is willing to sacrifice his relationship with his father rather than accept his father's love for his younger brother.

There are three consequences of bitterness:

1. **Bitterness robs you of joy.** The older brother has no joy in his work or in knowing all his father has left will be his. This is significant because according to Jewish law and tradition, the oldest son would receive twice the inheritance of the younger son. Also, the older son

would not have to live with the memories of all the sins and hurts of his younger brother. However, his bitterness has robbed him of the joy of all his blessings... Robert G. Menzies makes the statement: *"It is a simple but forgotten truth that the greatest enemy to present joy and high hopes is the cultivation of retrospective bitterness."* The older brother and many of us are examples of this truth.

2. **Bitterness causes you to self-destruct.** An excellent biblical example is Saul, the first king of Israel. He has everything going for him, good looks, popularity, talent, success, and power. But after the shepherd boy David slays the giant and returns home, the Israelites praised him by singing, "Saul have killed his thousands, and David ten-thousand" (1 Sam. 18;7b). In 1 Samuel 18:8a notice how Saul responds. The verse reads: *"Then Saul was very angry, and the saying displeased him."* Saul's anger boils over then turned into bitterness, and eats him up. Maya Angelou made the statement: "Bitterness is like cancer. It eats up the host." Saul's bitterness caused him to try to kill David on several occasions... Bitterness muddied Saul's thinking both spiritually and militarily... Finally, the Philistines defeated the Israelites in battle. They killed three of Saul's sons, including Jonathan, David's best friend... As a result, Saul asked his armor-bearer to kill him. When the armor-bearer refused; "Saul took a sword and fell on it" (1 Sam. 31:4c). The Philistines didn't cause Saul's death; it was his own bitterness that caused him to self-destruct.

3. **Bitterness alienates you from God.** Rather than get rid of his bitterness, the older brother is willing to sacrifice his relationship with his father. That's exactly what we do when we harbor bitterness in our hearts. In Ephesians 4:31, we are told to; "Let all bitterness, and wrath, and anger, and clamor, and evil speaking, be put away from you, with all malice." When you see a list in the Bible, always

pay attention to what is first. Bitterness is listed first in Eph. 4:31, because all the other sins are results of bitterness. Bitterness is a horrible sin because it has so many sinful tentacles, like an octopus. Bitterness is sin, or iniquity. You should therefore remember the words of Psalm 66:18; *"If I regard iniquity in my heart, the Lord will not hear."*

To defeat bitterness not only must you analyze the cause and realize the consequences, you must:

IV. UTLIZE THE CURE FOR YOUR BITTERNESS (LUKE 15:31-32).

"And he said to him, "Son, you are always with me, and all that I have is yours… It was right that we should make merry and be glad, for your brother was dead and is alive again, and was lost and is found."

The father who is the main character in this story, reminds the older son and brother of three thing for defeating bitterness;

1. Remember Who You Are:

The father reminds the son in 15:31a; "Son you are always with me." He reminds the "bitter" older brother that he is still his son and always will be. When you are tempted to become angry and bitter, you need to remember who you are and whose you are… As a believer, you are a child of God, and you should act like it. In spite of how things seem to be we are instructed in Philippians 2:15 to; *"Become blameless and harmless, children of God with fault in the midst a crooked and perverse generation among whom you shine as lights in the world."* Remembering who you are and whose you are helps you to realize there is no excuse for bitterness toward anyone.

2. Focus on God's Faithfulness:

Don't forget God will give you just what you deserve. While the prodigal son has been restored with a homecoming party, the fact remains he has wasted his inheritance (15:13). He will receive nothing that belongs to his older brother. Therefore, notice the words of the father to the bitter son in 15:31c; "All that I have is yours." The life lesson here is this, when you see people you think are undeserving succeed, or receive praise, don't feel cheated and become bitter. Live according to God's will, and you will get your just reward, because of God's faithfulness.

3. Do the Right Thing:

Notice what the words of the father to his oldest son in 15:32; *"It was right that we should make merry and be glad, for you brother was dead and is alive again, and was lost and is found."* The father will not cancel the party because it is the right thing to do... The younger brother's rebellion and sin brought him to ruin... He will receive no more inheritance. When the father dies, he will probably end up working for his older brother.

The older bitter brother needs to realize his life has been and will continue to be much better than that of his poor, disgraced brother... This one-day celebration will not change that... The celebration is the right thing to do, for it was truly a time of joy for the father and his family.

To utilize the cure for bitterness, remember who and whose you are, focus on God's faithfulness, and do the right thing... These stories of the "father and his two sons have no ending... Jesus doesn't tell us whether or not the older brother comes into the celebration. He leaves that decision up to you and me. Will you come into the Father's fellowship, or will you stay in the field of bitterness? You can defeat bitterness, by analyzing the cause, realizing the consequences, and utilizing the cure.